"From the moment I laid eyes on this study I knew it was something special. As a woman with a heart after God, I long to know Him even better and have searched for a practical tool like this. Daphne has taken deep, sacred concepts and created a simple, *absolutely delicious way to present truth to the heart* of the participant. What a gift this is for those who are thirsty for more of God!"

–Jan Goss-Gibson,
http://civilityconsulting.com, Austin, Texas

"When I did this study with Daphne, *it had a lasting impact on my life.* She helped me realize that I had to step out of my comfort zone to draw closer to God. To this day, her words are still with me!"

–Michelle Humphries,
Victoria, Texas

"Powerful study! It was a very difficult time in my life when I did this Bible study. It literally changed the course of my legacy. Daphne is an amazing mentor and I have personally witnessed countless lives changed through her Godly guidance. *This study delivers!*"

–Amanda Smalley,
Point Venture, Texas

"It was a blessing to participate in the pilot group for Daphne's 'Take Me Deeper Still' Bible Study. She assembled a group of loving, faithful women and together we learned so many amazing details about the Old and New Testaments. This extraordinary devotional book was developed with love and attention to detail. *This book is a must for everyone!"*

–Robbyn Michalka,
Victoria, Texas

"Daphne Zuniga's passion for drawing people to the Word of God is evident in this book. You will be encouraged, inspired, and will discover many hidden treasures of God's Word through this incredible study. *It is an honor to endorse this amazing resource."*

–Lori Champion,
Celebration Church, Georgetown, Texas.

"I was blessed to meet Daphne and Paul at my writing seminar in Austin, Texas this year. I learned of their ministry and God's call on their lives. Daphne shared with me the manuscript you are holding. This is my 57th year in ministry and I have seen many "helps" for the body of Christ. Frankly, many of them are "surface material." This book is different. It contains a wealth of God's wisdom; and for we busy people, Daphne has skillfully laid out in "bite-size" pieces that will lead us to a deeper relationship with the Father. *I encourage you to spend the next 40 days with Daphne and the Father, and be transformed."*

–Eddie Smith,
Co-founder & President, U.S. Prayer Center, Houston, Texas

Take Me Deeper Still

40 Days to a Closer Walk with God

DAPHNE ZUNIGA

http://www.Daphnez.com
7710-T Cherry Park Dr, Ste 224
Houston, TX 77095
713-766-4271

Paperback: 978-1-68411-197-8

Hardcover: 978-1-68411-261-6

Dedication

I dedicate this book to all the people who have shaped my walk with Christ:

*To my **parents**, who took me to church every Sunday morning, Sunday night and Wednesday night. I may have acted like a heathen, but something stuck!*

*To my **sister** who forever influenced my life in 2001 when she told me that God was not satisfied with the wife that I had been. Though I was irritated at the time, I treasure those words more than you will ever know!*

*To **Cindy Staley**, who held my hand during the hardest time of my life and introduced me to the New Covenant!*

*To **Ms. Joan**, who met with me almost every Friday for 4 years and taught me how to live a Christ-Centered life. I am glad I did not follow through all the times I wanted to fire you, because you told me what I needed to hear and not what I wanted to hear. You changed my life forever.*

*To our two children, **David** and **Avery**, who are gifts from God. You both delight my heart and I love to watch you grow in the Lord.*

*And most of all, I dedicate this book to my amazing husband, **Paul**, the man God chose to use to make me the woman I am today. My love for you deepens every day and I consider myself blessed to have you.*

Acknowledgements

In 2007, I invited a group of women from my church to go through a Bible Study that God placed on my heart. Amanda, Holly, Robbyn, Georgette, Nona, Michelle, Melissa, Barbara and Kelly all agreed and we met every Saturday for six weeks. I am eternally grateful for their wisdom, insight, commitment, friendship and love.

I thank Jan Goss-Gibson and her husband Rick Gibson. Being in your Vineyard Mastermind Group has given us direction, discipline and confidence to make our dreams into a reality. We love and appreciate you both! Thank you Jan for loving this study!

I would not have published this Bible Study at all were it not for my husband Paul Zuniga. Though I wrote the study in 2007, I did not intend to publish it until he read it in 2016. He insisted that we publish it and made numerous improvements. Paul, thank you so much for encouraging me to publish this Bible Study and for your tireless hours of assisting with the process.

Finally, I would like to thank David Whitehead, our editor. David, it is with tears of overflowing gratitude that I write this. Each time you sent an email telling me how much people need this study and how much it impacted you personally while you were editing I was humbled. Your encouraging emails further confirm that God wanted this to be written *and* published. Thank you for your input, guidance and the friendship that we have developed because of this process. Because of you, we are ready to embark on our next book!

Contents

Dedication v

Acknowledgements................................. vii

Contents.. ix

Foreword xiii

Introduction... xvii

Day 1 – Seeking God 1

Day 2 – Take Charge 5

Day 3 – Noah (Part 1)................................... 9

Day 4 – Noah (Part 2)................................. 11

Day 5 – Abram (Part 1) 15

Day 6 – Abram (Part 2) 19

Day 7 – Abram becomes Abraham (Part 3) 23

Day 8 – Isaac and Jacob 27

Day 9 – Jacob 31

Day 10 – Joseph... 35

Day 11 – Moses (Part 1) 39

Day 12 – Moses (Part 2) 41

Day 13 – Moses (Part 3) 45

Day 14 – Moses and Joshua 49

Day 15 – Review 53

Day 16 – Joshua 55

Day 17 – Ruth 59

Day 18 – Saul and David (Part 1) 63

Day 19 – David (Part 2) 67

Day 20 – David (Part 3) 71

Day 21 – David (Part 4) 75

Day 22 – David and Solomon 80

Day 23 – King Solomon 86

Day 24 – Ezra 91

Day 25 – Nehemiah.. 95

Day 26 – Daniel 99

Day 27 – Old Testament 105

Day 28 – Our Savior is Born 109

Day 29 – John the Baptist Prepares the Way 115

Day 30 – The Beginning of Jesus' Ministry 119

Day 31 – The Life and Teachings of Our Savior 125

Day 32 – The Life and Teachings of Our Savior 129

Day 33 – The Final Teachings of Our Savior 133

Day 34 – The Final Teachings of Our Savior 137

Day 35 – The Final Hours of Christ 143

Day 36 – The Final Hours of Christ 147

Day 37 – Christ's Final Prayer 153

Day 38 – Completion 155

Day 39 – Resurrection 161

Day 40 – Ascension of Christ and the Holy Spirit 165

Conclusion 169

Author's Page 171

Foreword

Do you understand the Bible? Do you have a deep knowledge of the lessons contained in the greatest book ever written?

We all know the basic premise of the Bible and the general story line. However, do we really know the Bible? Do we have a grasp of how these events led up to the ultimate action of the crucifixion and resurrection of Jesus?

I always felt that I had a basic understanding of the Bible and the events contained between the front and back cover but I wanted to know more. I did not know how to go about it though, other than just sitting down and reading through it page by page until the pieces fit together and made sense.

I sat in church for years and wondered how all of the Scriptures tied together. I wondered about the lineage of the people in the Bible. I struggled to understand the geography in the Bible. There seemed to be so much information to learn and the different translations intimidated me even more.

I watched in awe as others turned so quickly to certain chapters of the Bible when the Pastor asked them to do so. I lacked the special talent that others had to be able to flip right to specific Scriptures.

I thought one day I would have this awakening and I would miraculously be able to do those things with little or no effort. I thought understanding of everything in the Scriptures would suddenly come to me and it would all make sense. Of course, I later discovered this was not the case.

Understanding the Scriptures takes time and effort. It requires study and dedication to come to the place where the interwoven threads within become apparent. However, if we present those deep truths in clear and concise ways, one can identify and understand them easier and faster. That is where this Bible Study comes in.

From the beginning of the Old Testament to the end of the New Testament, this study will help you see how the entire story fits together so that it will make perfect sense. It will springboard you into a better understanding of how it affects your life, so you can live the way Jesus wants you to live, and enjoy the riches of a deeper walk with Him.

I have to tell you the story about how this masterpiece became available to you:

My wife, Daphne, wrote this Bible Study for women in 2007. She gathered some friends from church and they all went through it as a group. There were special moments that they shared during that time and all of those wonderful women grew closer to Christ.

The study was placed on a shelf for a few months, then ended up in a closet, then was packed in a box when we moved to Round Rock, Texas in 2012. That box sat forgotten in a closet in our home office until 2016 when we discovered it while cleaning.

Daphne almost cried when she found it because she thought it had been lost in the move. She thumbed through it for a few days and then handed it to me. She knew I needed some help with my spiritual walk and she thought that reading through this study might help me.

I knew that she had written it and I knew that she went through the lessons with that first group of women, but I didn't appreciate the effort and love she put into the development of the manuscript and had never taken the time to look at it until then.

It blew me away when I read it.

She did not intend to publish it as a book when she wrote it. She just felt God prompting her to do something for His glory. She felt that He was telling her that women needed something to help them with their spiritual walk. After I read it, I told her to publish it and that she could not limit it to women because men could benefit from it as well (After all, it would not have been fair to the men in this world).

I told Daphne this Bible Study was the best we had ever produced. Her response was typical, but genuine. She said that the words were not hers; they were from God.

I agree wholeheartedly!

Paul Zuniga

Introduction

It is a privilege and an honor to have you join us in this Bible Study. We pray that God will touch your life and challenge you in ways that you never thought possible.

This Bible Study is straight forward, and *created to increase your hunger for God's Presence in your life, and to instill in you a desire for a deeper, closer walk with Him.* It requires daily diligence, simple faith and a loving commitment to be obedient to God's Word.

The Bible Study consists of 40 days of lessons. You will experience the joy of deepening your relationship with God on several levels each day of the Bible Study.

Each lesson will include:

A *Prayer* to begin the session by immediately connecting to God

A *Lesson* in God's Word with *Exercises* to deepen your understanding

Memorization of the names of the Books of the Bible (taken in small steps)

A final *Prayer of Agreement* to seal what you have learned into your heart

You will need a few things to get started:

A Bible, preferably *The Message* version, as we are using this version in the Bible Study

A *Bible Highlighter* (be sure it's not the kind that will bleed through the pages)

A small *Journal* for recording your thoughts and prayers throughout the day and for extra space if you need more writing room when answering questions based on our Bible Readings

Index Cards for memorizing the Books of the Bible (You will use the first for the five Books of the Law. You will use the second for the 12 Historical Books. You will use the third for the five Books of Wisdom. You will use the fourth for the 17 Books of the Prophets. The fifth, sixth and seventh cards will be used for the 27 books of the New Testament.

Pen or *Pencil* Our desire is that during the course of this Bible Study you will memorize the order of the Books of the Bible, understand the significance of God's Covenant Agreements, learn to discern God's prompting, and learn how to put action to your faith by abandoning yourself and allowing God to use you.

We hope you are prepared for the divine adventure you are about to embark upon. Your participation demonstrates a longing to enter into a deeper relationship with Christ. He is ready and waiting for your undivided attention. If you will approach every session anticipating a deeper walk with Him, then you will not be disappointed!

Allow us to pray for you right now:

Heavenly Father, I pray for my reader who is entering into this Bible Study. Strengthen him with might by Your Holy Spirit, and show him the depths of your love. Reveal more of yourself to him, as he comes to know you more and more. In the name of Jesus I pray, Amen.

Day 1

OPENING PRAYER

*L*ord, *You say in Your Word that if I seek, then I will find. I set myself today to seek You and I stand in faith that I will find You. As I pursue You in prayer and in Your Word, I thank You that my walk with You is being strengthened, and that my relationship with You is deepening each and every day. In the name of Jesus I pray, Amen.*

LESSON: SEEKING GOD

Seeking and knowing God is the most important pursuit in your Christian walk after being saved, baptized, and filled with the Holy Spirit. In fact, it *is* your Christian walk.

Jesus said it best when He prayed His final prayer before He was seized and captured in John 17:1-5 (Please turn there in your Bible; read and highlight).

Notice that He said, *"And this is the real and eternal life: That they know You, the one and only true God, and Jesus Christ, Whom You sent."*

God has a purpose and a plan for your life. Turn to Jeremiah 29:11 and see how it confirms this. In order for Him to reveal this plan, you must enter into a deep relationship with Him and seek Him.

One of the main definitions in the Merriam-Webster Dictionary of the word _seek_ is _"to go in search of."_ An additional definition of the word is found in Dr. James Strong's Concordance. Dr. Strong's Concordance, first written in 1890, assists with further understanding of the original Hebrew and Greek words (The original manuscripts of the Books of the Bible were in Hebrew and Greek).

One of the Greek definitions for the word _seek_ is _"to seek out for one's self, beg, crave."_ Putting both definitions together - let us go in search of God, _begging_ to know Him deeper and _craving_ a more meaningful relationship with Him.

In this Bible Study, we are going in search of the one and only true God. We will begin seeking God in the Old Testament where we will see how God forms relationships based on Covenant Agreements. God's perfect plan of salvation, seen in the Old Testament, comes alive in the New Testament. We will observe how the saints of the Old and New Testaments sought after God and found Him. We will then do what they did and we will come to know God deeply, and we will know Him _deeper still_.

LESSON EXERCISES

(Write your answers and your notes in your journal and do not forget to highlight what is meaningful to you!)

1.) Review John 17:1-5

What does it say the _"real and eternal life"_ is?

2.) Read and highlight Deuteronomy 4:29-31

When looking for God, you must look for Him with your entire _____ and _____.

What is it God will not forget about?

3.) Read and highlight 1 Chronicles 16:8-19

List five things this passage tells you to do.

4.) Read and highlight 2 Chronicles 15:1-6 and 2 Chronicles 15:10-15

What is the main point of these two passages?

5.) Read and highlight Isaiah 45:18-24

List three things God said are true about Him and three things He said are not true about Him.

6.) Read and highlight Isaiah 55:1-7

List four rewards for seeking God.

7.) Read and highlight Proverbs 28:5

What will those who seek God know inside and out?

MEMORIZATION

Beginning tomorrow, you will start memorizing the names of the Books of the Bible a few at a time, but for today, look up the Table of Contents of your Bible and familiarize yourself with them. Read them at least once and say each one aloud.

PRAYER OF AGREEMENT

Read and Highlight Matthew 18:18-20. Just as Jesus said to take it seriously, we take that passage seriously here and now, and enter into a prayer of agreement with you.

Father, thank You for my reader. Richly bless and prosper our time together in this study as we seek to know You in a deeper way. Reveal the real and eternal life to us, and help us seek you with all of our hearts. May we come to know and fulfill Your plan for our lives. In the name of Jesus I pray, Amen.

Day 2

OPENING PRAYER

*L*ord, I am anticipating You during this study and I am eager to learn the things that You want me to know. Please open my heart and my mind as I prepare for Your lessons, and strengthen my ability to apply them in my life. In the name of Jesus I pray, Amen.

LESSON: TAKE CHARGE

One night I woke up to a loud thunderstorm. After tossing and turning, I decided to get up and read. I picked up my copy of *The Message* version of the Bible and turned to the very beginning. I read and highlighted the Introduction, written by Eugene Peterson, where he explained his reason for putting together this version, which was to get more people to read their Bible.

I am so glad I took the time to read his introduction because it created a new hunger in me to know God's Word and to have a deeper understanding of it. I found many wonderful nuggets from God's Word that stormy night; even from the passages, I had read many times before, but I now saw in a new and exciting way. I pray that you have the same experience as you read and highlight your Message Bible. Let us begin our adventure in the word in the Old Testament.

Many Christians do not understand the relevance of the Old Testament in their lives today. The Old Testament used to overwhelm me and I failed to see a direct connection between it and my life. However, as I began to take the time to read and understand the Old Testament, I realized how very wrong I had been. *The Old Testament is critical when it comes to knowing God.*

I always thought the New Testament was the only part of the Bible about Jesus, but after studying the Old Testament, I learned that it was all about Him too. In fact, Jesus Himself said so when He met two disciples on the way to Emmaus who had come to doubt Him after His death in Luke 24:25-27:

"Then He said to them, "So thick-headed! So slow-hearted! Why can't you believe all that the prophets said? Don't you see that these things had to happen, that the Messiah had to suffer and only then enter into His glory?" Then He started at the beginning, with the Books of Moses, and went on through all the Prophets, pointing out everything in the Scriptures that referred to Him."

What Jesus did that day was expound on every book of the Old Testament and their prophecies and demonstrate how they all spoke of Him, His coming, and His nature. He proved to them that He and He alone had fulfilled the Old Testament prophecies. Once we realize this, the Old Testament will come alive for us!

Begin today by reading and highlighting Genesis 1:26-28.

If we are going to know the one true God, we need to look at ourselves and see that He made us in His image and have His nature.

Write down the four directives that God gave to humankind to bless them.

Now, take a peek at Genesis 1:23. What one blessing did God give human beings that He did not give the fish and the birds?

Some translations say we "have dominion over the earth." Others say we "rule over the earth." I like the way the Message Bible says it: *"Take Charge!"*

LESSON EXERCISES

(Write out your answers and your notes and do not forget to highlight what is meaningful to you!)

List at least one reason the Old Testament is important to read and study

When God says He made us in His Image, what does that mean to you?

If you feel bad about yourself and criticize the way you look, have you accepted and realized that God made you in His image?

When God says He gave us His nature, what does that mean to you?

God created us to Take Charge. What does this mean to you?

If we allow circumstances to rule us, have we taken charge?

What are some things in your life that you need to take charge of in order to raise the standards of your life to reflect His nature?

MEMORIZATION

As we discussed we will be memorizing a few of the Books of the Bible each day. Please get your first index card and write "Books of the Law" at the top. Number the card from 1-5 and write the names of the first two Books of the Bible, Genesis and Exodus, beside numbers one and two.

PRAYER OF AGREEMENT

Father, Reveal to my reader and me more concerning the truth that we have been created in Your image. Help us take on Your nature in every area of our lives and take charge of all You have set to be under our dominion. In the name of Jesus I pray, Amen.

Day 3

OPENING PRAYER

*L*ord, *I am asking you to move in my heart today as I give myself to You, and I thank You in advance for guiding all my steps and keeping me in Your will. I submit myself to Your Holy Spirit and Your teaching in all circumstances. In the name of Jesus I pray, Amen.*

LESSON: NOAH (PART 1)

Read and highlight today's main text: Genesis 6:5-22, with emphasis on verses 8-10 and verse 22.

At this point in history, the earth had become filled with evil and nothing but evil. However, God found one good man – Noah. Therefore, God gave Noah a mission to preserve the species of the earth and to preserve the human race. Verse 8 tells us that God liked what He saw in Noah. Noah lived his life the way God had intended for man to live; according to His divine nature. If you had lived in the time of Noah, would God have found the same things in you that He found in Noah?

LESSON EXERCISES

Name three things about Noah that were pleasing to God.

Name three personal attributes you possess that are pleasing to God.

MEMORIZATION

Write down the names of the next three Books of the Bible - Leviticus, Numbers and Deuteronomy, on your index card that you made yesterday. There should now be the names of all five of the first Books of the Bible on your card. These five books are "The Books of Moses" or "The Books of the Law." Say them aloud several times throughout the day until you have them memorized.

PRAYER OF AGREEMENT

Father, bless and prosper my reader and me as we continue in this Bible study and learn to be like Noah in our world. Give us peace of mind, knowing that as long as we endeavor to walk with You as Noah did, we will find favor in your sight. In the name of Jesus I pray, Amen.

Day 4

OPENING PRAYER

Heavenly Father, please help me today to walk by Your Word and not my own feelings. I set myself in faith to do as You would have me do, say what You would have me say, and think what You would have me think. In the name of Jesus I pray, Amen.

LESSON: OLD TESTAMENT COVENANTS – NOAH (PART 2)

The very foundation of our relationship to God is through "Covenant Agreements." Because of humankind's rebellion, his relationship to God was shattered. God instituted Covenant Agreements as His way of restoring that broken relationship. A Covenant Agreement is a simple binding contract between two parties.

Throughout this Bible Study, we will pull back the curtain on these Covenants in the Old Testament and reveal their significance when it comes to how God deals with His people, and we will explore how, through these Covenants and the Prophets, God brought about His New and Everlasting Covenant through Christ Jesus.

Let us begin today's lesson by reading and highlighting Genesis 8:20-21.

What did God vow never to do again?

Now read and highlight Genesis 9:1-17.

We learned yesterday that Noah did absolutely everything that God commanded him to do. After the water receded, Noah and his family and all of the animals disembarked from the Ark, and Noah built an altar on which he offered burnt offerings to God. God blessed Noah and his family by giving them the same directives He had given Adam and Eve: *"Prosper! Reproduce! Fill the Earth!"*

Then in verses 8-11, He established the very first Covenant Agreement.

It is astonishing that the very symbol Noah saw that day, the symbol of the Rainbow, we can still see today. I love this constant reminder of His Covenant Agreement with us.

LESSON EXERCISES

With what three groups did God make His Covenant?

God summarizes these groups in verse 17. With whom does He say He is making this Covenant?

What sign did God establish to remind mankind of His Covenant?

MEMORIZATION

Review all five of the Books of Moses and make sure you know them.

PRAYER OF AGREEMENT

Lord, Your Word says that we have only to come to You in believing prayer and we will have what we ask from You. Grant us wisdom and guidance today. Reveal Your plan to us, and light our path. In the name of Jesus I pray, Amen.

Day 5

OPENING PRAYER

Dear Lord, as I get ready to spend time in Your Word and do my study today, I submit to You and Your will for my life. I submit to You as a piece of clay submits to the potter, and I am trusting in You to fashion me into a vessel You can use to the fullest, in the name of Jesus, Amen.

LESSON: ABRAM (PART 1)

Read and highlight Genesis 12:1-9. Verses 1-3 are the "Abrahamic Covenant."

Approximately 4000 years ago, God disclosed His plans for the redemption of mankind to Abram; though Abram might not have understood it as such. God began by instructing Abram to leave his family and everything he knew, and journey to a land that God would show him. Abram left Haran, the wealthiest city in Mesopotamia, and his friends and relatives, to go to a place he had never been and had never seen.

God had plans to prosper Abram and to give him hope and a future. What were the specific promises God made to Abram in this passage?

God appeared to Abram five more times to reinforce the Covenant and go through the covenant rituals that Abram would expect. However, Abram did not question God; he chose to be obedient.

Has God disclosed plans for your future to you? Has He expected you to do something that sounded strange, or even crazy like the one He expected of Abram? (Just wait, He will!) Write down the things God has asked of you and the things He has promised to do for you. If you cannot think of any now, then ask Him to reveal them to you. Thank Him for revealing His will in your life.

Now, read and highlight Genesis 13:14-18.

God has shown Abram the land He has promised to him. In verse 17 God says, *"Here is the land that I promised, now on your feet, get moving!"*

Have you ever heard God speak that way?

There have been several times in my life that I felt God urging me the same way He did to Abram. However, often times my own fear and lack of understanding and belief paralyze me. What I have come to realize is that God does not require us to understand His plan. What He requires from us is that we obey and be thankful.

Abram is an excellent example of obedience to God. I am certain he dealt with fear just like us, but in faith he obeyed. Take a little time and write a prayer of thanksgiving for all that God has given you.

MEMORIZATION

Review the Books of Moses. Now, get out your second index card and label it at the top with "Historical Books". Number the card from 1-12, and then fill in the first three with the names of the first three Historical Books: Joshua, Judges and Ruth. Repeat them a few times.

PRAYER OF AGREEMENT

Father, we pray for strength to do what You ask us to do; especially anything out of the ordinary. Give us strength to be consistently obedient to You, even when we don't understand the full purpose of Your directives. In the name of Jesus I pray, Amen.

Day 6

OPENING PRAYER

God in Heaven, please help me today to keep my mind and thoughts on You and not on my circumstances. I trust in You to keep me in perfect peace, according to Your Word, and to lift me above all worldly worries, in the name of Jesus, Amen.

LESSON: ABRAM (PART 2)

Read and highlight Genesis 15:1-8.

God continued to tell Abram what He was going to do for him. He assured and comforted Abram. He told Abram in verse 1: "Don't be afraid, Abram. I'm your shield. Your reward will be grand!" Up to that point Abram listened and obeyed. Now he was beginning to question God's promise. It was confusing to Abram. God said He was going to make Abram the father of many nations, yet Abram had no children. Abram and Sarai were old.

Write down a summary of Abram's questions to God in Genesis 15:2-3.

Once again, God showed Abram the stars of the sky and promised him that just like the stars he will have so many descendants he will be unable to count them all.

Abram told God that he believed Him, but then Abram asked a very important question: *"Master God, how in the world am I to know this is mine?"*

God responded with something Abram understood: *A Blood Covenant.*

Abram instantly recognized that God was instructing him to go through the ceremonies of a binding contract between two parties that were very popular and very serious in Abram's day.

I must confess I did not understand the significance of the ceremonial Blood Covenant the first time I read this in the Bible. It was not until later that God revealed to me the beauty of this most enduring and sacred act.

Before God entered into the covenant, He told Abram what was to come. He did not promise Abram it was going to be easy; in fact, He told Abram that many of his descendants would live in slavery for four hundred years before fulfilling the promise. God's plan even prevented Abram from witnessing the fulfillment of God's promise himself.

Finally, God walked through the midst of the split animals signifying that He was cutting the covenant with Abram and bound Himself to His unconditional promise.

With this covenant, God established the basis by which He made all other covenants with His people. Can you see how God is laying the foundation of the New Covenant, which was fulfilled by Christ many years later?

LESSON EXERCISES

What animals did God tell Abram to bring for the Cutting of the Covenant?

According to Genesis 15:17, what two things did God appear as, as He passed through the midst of the split animals?

MEMORIZATION

Review the Books of Law that you memorized by Moses. Now review the first three Historical Books. Now write the names of the next two books on the same index card.

(1 Samuel and 2 Samuel) Continue to review them until you know them.

PRAYER OF AGREEMENT

Dear Lord, my reader and I ask You to strengthen us with might by Your Spirit in our inner being, that our love may abound more and more in knowledge and depth of insight. We pray this in the mighty name of Jesus, Amen.

Day 7

OPENING PRAYER

ather, may nothing separate me from You today. What a difference it makes when I put You first and make You my desire, instead of the things of this world. I purposely move closer to You, and I know You have promised that when I do You will move closer to me. I thank You for Your close presence, in the name of Jesus, Amen.

LESSON: ABRAM BECOMES ABRAHAM (PART 3)

God promised Abram that he would have many descendants, but Abram and his wife Sarai were elderly and quite along in years, this was going to require real faith. In Genesis 16 we find that after some time had passed Sarai was getting frustrated that she seemed unable to provide Abram with a son.

She did what most of us have done – she decided to help God out a little.

Sarai told Abram to sleep with her maid in order to provide him a son. Abram seemed okay with this (I would like to say a few things to Abram at this point) and he slept with the maid. Once the maid, whose name was "Hagar" realized she was pregnant, she got an attitude and "looked down on her mistress (Sarai).

Sarai abused Hagar, and Hagar ran away. God went to Hagar and, in His mercy, promised to give her many descendants if she would return to Sarai. She did as God told her to and went back to Sarai, and soon after that gave birth to a son, she named "Ishmael" as God had instructed.

Now, read and highlight Genesis 17.

Even after Abram and Sarai had decided to take things into their own hands, God extended gentle grace to them. It had been 24 years since Abram first heard from God, and again God went to Abram and reiterated His promise to him. God confirmed His covenant with Abram by fulfilling three more of the Blood Covenant ceremonies:

First, God recited His covenant vows aloud and elaborated on His spoken promises.

Second, God exchanged names with Abram and Sarai, and told Abram his name will now be Abraham, which means "Father of Many Nations" and that Sarai will now be Sarah. (Later we learn from that point on, God calls Himself "The God of Abraham")

Third, circumcision sealed His promise. This symbolized God cutting His covenant into their bodies as *"a permanent mark of My permanent covenant."*

Now, fast forward to Genesis 21:1 where *"God did for Sarah what He promised: Sarah became pregnant and gave Abraham a son in his old age, and at the very time God had set."* Abraham named his new son Isaac. As God instructed, Abraham circumcised Isaac when he was eight days old.

Because Abraham was diligent and faithfully held on to God's promise, he received his heart's desire. With the birth of Isaac, the fulfilling of God's promise had begun.

LESSON EXERCISES

Abram and Sarai made a mistake when they attempted to help God work His miracle and bring them a son. Have you tried to "help" God before? I have attempted to help Him many times and failed. What did you do to help God, and what did you learn from it?

Abram and Sarai's attempt to "help" God resulted in the birth of Ishmael, the father of the Arabs. There has been a struggle between the descendants of Isaac and Ishmael ever since.

MEMORIZATION

Please review the first ten Books of the Bible you wrote on your index cards. Write the names of the 11th and 12th books, (the sixth and seventh on this card) 1 & 2 Kings, on the Historical Books index card. Recite them until you feel you know them.

PRAYER OF AGREEMENT

O God, grant my reader and I a deeper knowledge of every aspect of Your character as we delve deeper into this study. Great I Am, reveal more of yourself to us. In the name of Jesus, Amen.

Day 8

OPENING PRAYER

*L*ord, *I desire a more intimate relationship with You. I long to know You more and more, and to see Your face. I ask You to reveal more of Yourself as I seek You, and as I study Your Word and spend quiet time with You. Take me deeper Jesus! It is in Your name I pray, Amen.*

LESSON: ISAAC AND JACOB

Read and highlight Genesis 25:21-26.

Isaac married Rebekah and he carried on his father Abraham's legacy by seeking God. Describe how Isaac prays to God in verse 21.

Isaac prayed hard for Rebekah, petitioning God for a deep desire that he and his wife both had. God answered Isaacs's prayer and Rebekah became pregnant. God told Rebekah that she will give birth to two nations and the older will serve the younger. She gave birth and Esau came first, followed by Jacob. The custom of the times was that the younger son would serve the first born, the older son. However, God is setting the stage and He informed Rebekah that Esau would serve Jacob. God chose Jacob to be the one through which He would carry out the covenant.

The Bible has many amazing testimonies of individual lives. I confess I spent much of my life thinking that the Bible was full of honest, upright people. When I stopped living vicariously through other people's interpretation of the Bible, and began reading it for myself, I learned that it is more like reality television.

Cain killed Abel and acted as if he had not, Abram slept with his maidservant, and in Genesis 27 Isaac, in his old age – blind, confused and fooled by Rebekah gave the blessing to Jacob believing he was giving it to Esau. What a story! The tabloids would pay millions for those stories today.

Read and highlight Genesis 28:3-4. In your Journal, write down the blessing Isaac gave Jacob.

God reassured Jacob of his inheritance in Genesis 28:10-22. Read and highlight this passage.

When God showed up it changed Jacob. He was in awe of God. He could hardly believe God was with him. Has there been a time in your life when you felt you were going along all by yourself and then God showed up?

Just like Jacob, my prayer and hope is that you *do* want to exclaim *"Incredible! Wonderful! ... Holy."* Take time to reflect on the majesty of God and how incredible it is that are able to understand what Jacob experienced thousands of years ago.

MEMORIZATION

Add 1 & 2 Chronicles to your index card. Review all 14 books until you know them. Keep up the good work!

PRAYER OF AGREEMENT

Lord, may my reader and I experience as powerful a meeting with you as Jacob did, so we can exclaim as he did that You are awesome, wonderful, and holy. Show Yourself to us Lord, and let us experience the fullness of your presence. In the name of Jesus, Amen.

Day 9

OPENING PRAYER

*F*ather, help me to see the opportunities to share You and Your *Word with others today. I submit myself as a vessel or tool in Your mighty hand; use me to bless others and spread Your Word and Your wisdom, Your healing power and Your ability to deliver hurting people from darkness, in the name of Jesus, Amen.*

LESSON: JACOB

When we are truly seeking God, we must take time to stop and listen. He makes many requests of us repeatedly. He often makes those requests known through many different sources. Look at how many times God repeated the original promise He made to Abraham. Each generation of Abraham's descendants knew that God called Abraham "The Father of Many Nations" and that they would be receiving the Promised Land one day.

Read and highlight Genesis 32:9-12. Write the final statement of that passage in your Journal.

If you have ever had a problem with reminding God of His Word, then let this passage reassure you that God delights in the fact that you trust His Word enough to bring it up to Him.

Jacob prayed this for a very important reason. He was afraid of what his brother was going to do to him. Remember, Jacob had obtained the blessings that Isaac intended for Esau. Not surprisingly, Esau carried a grudge. He was VERY angry at Jacob and the Bible tells us that he sought to kill Jacob. Now that Jacob was going home, he sent word to Esau, and he has just learned that Esau was coming... with four hundred men!

Once he heard *that*, Jacob sought God fervently. Jacob then took his family to safety and prepared to meet his brother the next day.

Now read and highlight Genesis 32:24-32.

That night, the Bible tells us, Jacob wrestled with a man. That man was God. Actually, it was an angel of the Lord wrestling on behalf of God.

The symbolic significance of this is that Jacob had lived a life of wrestling; even from the womb, he had wrestled with his brother, he had later wrestled with his father in law, he had wrestled in life, and finally he found himself wrestling with God. Jacob might think he can wrestle with God, but God debilitated him, demonstrating to Jacob that God holds his destiny. Jacob finally acknowledged God was his source of strength when the angel of God said, *"let me go"* and Jacob replied *"Not until you bless me."*

God changed Jacob's name that day from Jacob to "Israel", which means "God-Wrestler." I find it fascinating that this is where the nation of Israel got its name and its character.

Read and highlight Genesis 35:9-12. God confirmed Jacob's name change to Israel and He reassured Jacob of the promise He made to Abraham and Isaac. Later, when Jacob met with Esau, Esau greeted Jacob warmly and guided him safely back to Canaan to their father, Isaac.

LESSON EXERCISES

Are there times when you have wrestled with God; perhaps with following one of His directives or believing one of His claims? List them. What helped you to stop wrestling?

Write down what you think He might change your name to and why:

MEMORIZATION

Please add Ezra, Nehemiah and Esther to your History Books card. This card is complete now! Memorize them and praise God there are only two more cards for the Old Testament. You are doing great!

PRAYER OF AGREEMENT

Lord, my reader and I ask today for Your peace and for peace of mind. We thank You for allowing us to enter into Your rest. We choose to trust and obey You, rather than to wrestle. Be God in every circumstance of our lives. In the name of Jesus I pray, Amen.

Day 10

OPENING PRAYER

*M*y Father in Heaven, I ask You to teach me to be a shining light in dark places. While others may wish to have an easy road, I ask You to give me the courage to reach into the places where people are hurting the most, and bring them Your light. Help me to always give You the glory, and to have the strength to stand against all the attacks of the enemy, in the name of Jesus I pray, Amen

LESSON: JOSEPH

Read and highlight Genesis chapter 37.

Jacob had 12 sons, but he made it clear that Joseph was his favorite (do not take parenting lessons from him!). As you can imagine this did not go over well with the other sons. Joseph's brothers became jealous, which only intensified when Joseph told his brothers about the dreams he had which predicted he would be a ruler over them. The brothers got so mad that they sold Joseph into slavery. Jacob had a beautiful coat made for Joseph and the brothers took that coat, killed a goat, put the goat's blood on it, and took it to Jacob. They told him that an angry pack of wild animals killed Joseph. Israel was so sad that he vowed to go to his grave mourning the loss of his favorite son.

Read and highlight Genesis chapter 39.

Joseph is now living with Potiphar and is *"one of Pharaoh's officials and the manager of his household."* Verse 2 says, *"As it turned out, God was with Joseph and things went very well with him."* Potiphar realized that God was with Joseph and put him in charge of many things. List some of the things he put under Joseph's care.

Because of his faith in God Joseph had a good thing going there with Potiphar, but it seems that all good things must come to an end, and Potiphar's wife frames Joseph by saying that he had raped her, when in fact he refused to touch her in any way. This landed Joseph in jail.

Again, God was with Joseph, and just as in Potiphar's house, Joseph wound up running the jail.

Dear friend, God is with you too.

He is with you just as He was with Joseph and His desire is to bless you and turn your situation around the same way. Are you struggling with circumstances right now?

Perhaps you have a difficult marriage, or are single and long for a happy marriage. Terrible things may have taken place in your life that were undeserved. Can you see that God is right there saying *"Don't worry about that I have so much more in store for you? This is just going to help your circumstances later. Hang on, I am showing you kindness in this situation. Look for Me and you will find Me."* When things seem worse than ever - think of Joseph.

Read and highlight Genesis chapters 40 and 41.

While in jail, Joseph sought God to interpret the dreams of the Head Baker and Head Cupbearer. His interpretation of both dreams was true. However, it was two full years later when Pharaoh had a dream that the Head Cupbearer remembered Joseph's accurate interpretation and told Pharaoh. Pharaoh sent for Joseph and told him that he had been informed that Joseph could interpret dreams. Read, highlight and record Joseph's response in Genesis 41:16.

Joseph made sure God got the glory and not him.

Joseph informed Pharaoh that God sent the dream and it showed that in a 14-year period there would be seven years of plenty and seven years of famine. Pharaoh put Joseph in charge of all Egypt, saying, *"you're the man for us. God has given you the inside story-no one is as qualified as you in experience and wisdom."*

Even though Joseph's brothers sold Joseph into slavery, and he was framed for a crime, God was still with Joseph, so much so, that Joseph was put in charge of all Potiphar's house, then later he was in charge of the jail, and finally, he was put in charge of all Egypt.

When the famine hit, Egypt had plenty of provisions because of Joseph's diligence. People from all over came to get the food Joseph stored during the years of plenty. Even Joseph's brothers from Canaan came. Bowing down to him, they did not recognize him, but he knew who they were and he realized it fulfilled the dream he had many years earlier. He ended up confronting and forgiving his brothers and reunited with his father Jacob. Pharaoh allowed all of Joseph's family to move to Egypt and *"made them the proud owners of choice land."*

Joseph never let circumstances interfere with God's plan. He trusted God, and always gave God the glory.

LESSON EXERCISES

What were the dreams of the Head Baker and Head Cupbearer?

Which one of them lived?

What were Pharaoh's dreams?

How were Josephs dreams from earlier in the story fulfilled?

MEMORIZATION

Now we are at the five Books of Wisdom. Use your third index card and write Books of Wisdom at the top. Then begin with your first two - Job and Psalms. Review all the books you have so far. Great job!

PRAYER OF AGREEMENT

Lord, my reader and I give You all the glory and choose to keep our eyes on You as You reveal what You are placing in our charge. Like Joseph, we ask You to use us mightily and fulfill all of our dreams. In Jesus' name, Amen.

Day 11

OPENING PRAYER

Dear Heavenly Father, help me to remember what a difference it makes when I put You first in my life. I set myself to always make You and Your Word the priority of my to do list each and every day. In Jesus' name, Amen.

LESSON: MOSES (PART 1)

What an amazing journey we have been on so far. We have seen dramatic scandals, demoralizing defeats and incredible victories. We have also seen the promise to Abraham handed down to Isaac, from Isaac to Jacob and from Jacob to Joseph and his brothers.

Just as God had warned Abraham, the Egyptians enslaved the Israelites after the death of Joseph, and their enslavement went on for 400 years. Just when many had given up hope and it looked as if the promise had been nothing but a dream, God remembered His covenant with Abraham, Isaac, and Jacob and He sent a deliverer.

That deliverer was Moses.

Moses was born to a family descended from Levi, one of Jacob's 12 sons. After Joseph and his brothers died, the children of Israel continued to reproduce. Pharaoh ordered the Egyptians to drown the Hebrew babies in order to control the Israelites and their population growth. The mother of Moses attempted to hide him. Pharaoh's daughter found Moses, and adopted him.

LESSON EXERCISES

Read and highlight Exodus 2:11-22. Summarize what took place.

Now settle down for a little extra Bible reading in the rest of Exodus chapter 2 and all of chapters 3 and 4.

MEMORIZATION

We are still on the Books of Wisdom card. Please write Proverbs, Ecclesiastes, and Song of Solomon on your card, and review all the books you have so far.

PRAYER OF AGREEMENT

Lord, my reader and I thank You constantly remembering Your Covenant concerning us. Thank You for fulfilling it completely in our lives, in Jesus' name, Amen.

Day 12

OPENING PRAYER

Father, I enter into Your presence of grace and mercy with praise upon my lips and thanksgiving upon my heart. I know that I can enter into Your Holy of Holies at any time with any request because the Blood of Jesus covers me and makes me holy in Your presence. I will always come boldly to You, even when I mess up, because I am Your child. In the name of Jesus I pray, Amen.

LESSON: MOSES (PART 2)

As we continue our journey, we see that Moses did not want to be the man that God selected to deliver His people from Egypt. He did not think he was equipped. He did not think that anyone would believe or trust him.

I can totally identify with Moses; I worry about what people think and what they say and how they will respond to certain things. I forget that God is the one who orchestrates everything; not me. All He needs for me to do is get out of His way. He needs me to see that it is not about me, but about His plan. Can you relate?

Is there something in your life that you know God wants to use you for, but you continually get in His way? Do you continually ask Him, "Why me? I am not good enough, I am not smart enough, and I do not have influence." What I have observed in Scripture and in life is that God delights in selecting people that are not equipped so He can be their guide. He chooses the most unlikely candidates so His light will shine. He does not call the equipped. He equips the called!

Are you the most unlikely person for the task? If so, then you are perfect for God's plan! Trust in Him, not in your own abilities or understanding and He will guide your every move.

In Exodus 4:13 Moses pled with God for the fifth and final time to send someone else. God angrily told Moses that his brother Aaron could communicate for him. Moses agreed and He and Aaron told the leaders of Israel everything God had asked. They demonstrated the signs and wonders and the people believed. Next, they went to Pharaoh and explained that God had asked him to set the Israelites free so they could worship Him in the wilderness. Not only did Pharaoh say no, but also he instructed his staff to work the Israelites even harder to cure them of their laziness and whining.

Read and highlight Exodus 5:22-23. What does Moses say to God?

Is Moses bold with God or what? We could all get a little self-righteous here and ask why Moses does not seem to believe God. However, we have all questioned God at times. God was very patient with Moses and He continued to reassure him.

Read and highlight Exodus 6:1-13.

It's interesting that God told Moses He was "The Strong God" for Abraham, Isaac and Jacob, but for Moses His "name was

God, meaning, I-Am-Present." God was saying, "*Trust Me I am here. I am going to be with you as you leave this country.*" First Moses and Aaron had to convince Pharaoh to release the Israelites. God told them exactly what to do and He warned them that Pharaoh would not obey. Moses and Aaron followed God's instructions and just as God had predicted, Pharaoh did not listen. Therefore, God sent 10 plagues on the Egyptian people.

Look at the beginning line after the heading of each plague.

Before He sent each plague, God spoke to Moses. He gave Moses specific instructions for Pharaoh. Pharaoh promised to release the Israelites during each of the plagues, but then when God ended the plague, Pharaoh reneged and went back on his word. None of the plagues had any effect on the Israelites.

The 10th and final plague took the life of every firstborn from every house of Egypt. This is important because it represented the ultimate judgment on Egypt since all the hopes and dreams for each family rested on their firstborn son; this judgment encompassed the entire community - males, females and cattle. God was very specific and intentional about each plague.

Not only was He demonstrating His power to Pharaoh and all Egypt, God was also demonstrating to the Israelites that they were His chosen people and He was going to protect them. He told Moses that He wanted the Israelites to tell their children and grandchildren how God saved them from all the plagues of Egypt so that they would all know that He was God.

We will study the final plague in depth in our next session, but for now take a little time to review God's specific instructions to Moses before He sent each plague.

LESSON EXERCISES

God still speaks to us today. He has not changed. Are you listening to His instructions? Are you walking with Him? Are you seeking Him in every situation? Write a prayer thanking God for the many signs and wonders recorded in this section. Thank Him for His promises of deliverance and salvation.

MEMORIZATION

Congratulations on completing the Books of the Law card, Historical Books card, and Books of Wisdom card. Now you can start the fourth card by writing Books of the Prophets at the top. Number the card 1-12 with 1-6 on the left side and 7-12 in the middle. Please write the first three books – Isaiah, Jeremiah, and Lamentations. If you have fallen behind do not get discouraged, just go back and do them over if you need to.

PRAYER OF AGREEMENT

Father, deliver my reader and me from the enemy in all circumstances, from every device that the adversary would send against us. Thank You Lord for Your delivering power, in the mighty name of Jesus, Amen.

Day 13

OPENING PRAYER

*L*ord, today I bear my entire heart and soul to You. I hide nothing from You, and I hold back nothing from You. I hold myself up for complete inspection and submit to You to change everything within me that needs to be changed. Work in me all that You wish today, Lord. Amen.

LESSON: MOSES (PART 3)

I left the 10th plague for today so we would have plenty of time to discuss the fulfillment of God's promises to Abraham.

Once again, just as He had done with Abraham, God sealed this promise with a demonstration of the Blood Covenant. In Exodus 12, God was very clear to the Israelites about leaving a legacy of faith. First He said *"This will be a memorial day for you; you will celebrate it as a festival to God down through the generations, a fixed festival celebration to be observed always."* (Exodus 12:14) He also tells them *"Keep this word. It is the law for you and your children, forever. When you enter the land which GOD will give you as He promised, keep doing this. In addition, when your children say to you, "Why are we doing this?' tell them: It's the Passover-sacrifice to God who passed over the homes of the Israelites in Egypt when He hit Egypt with death but rescued us"* (Exodus 12:24-27).

God did not want them to forget what He did. He wanted to make sure the Israelites passed the story down from generation to generation of how He set them free. The amazing part of this story is that it had been 430 years since God revealed His plan to Abraham and the Israelites had been passing *that* story down through the generations. Now they would have a new story to pass down – How God *kept* His promise.

The Passover played a considerable role in the lives of the Israelites. Remember that the blood covenant symbolized the substitution of one life for another. God had them take the life of a lamb without defect in order to save their own lives. There is a profound connection here. This event foreshadowed God's sacrifice of His unblemished Son, Jesus.

As God promised, the final plague came and the Israelites were unharmed. Pharaoh urged Moses and Aaron to leave and worship God as they initially requested. Pharaoh once again went back on his word and sent his army to bring the Israelites back to Egypt. Read and highlight Exodus 14:15-31. Record briefly what took place.

I love the last statement: *"The people were in reverent awe before God and trusted in God and his servant Moses".* Interestingly enough it did not take long before they doubted Moses *and* God. Read and highlight Exodus 15:22-27. Pay particular attention to verse 26. In Exodus 16:1-3 the complaining and doubting began. The Israelites were hungry and felt betrayed. They wanted to go back to the "comforts" of Egypt. Before we judge them, let us ask ourselves if we might have all done the exact same thing. It may

46

be that we have done the same thing in our lives at one time or another.

I think it is amazing that we can see and experience God's miracles and know He is with us, and then something comes along and knocks the wind out of our sail and causes us to doubt the very God who rescued us repeatedly. We are no better than the Israelites. Think of a time when you knew that you were in God's will. You were doing exactly as He requested, but then something caused you to doubt and you spiraled down that dark lonely road until you could go no more. What did God do to help you? What was your manna and quail? Was it a book? Was it a person? Record a time when God rescued you. What was the ultimate outcome?

LESSON EXERCISES

Thank God for His provision today. If you are still hungry for God's Word read and highlight Exodus chapter 16.

MEMORIZATION

Review all the Books of the Bible up to this point. Now add Ezekiel and Daniel to your list. Keep up the great work!

PRAYER OF AGREEMENT

Lord God, thank You for loving us. Bless my reader and myself, and our families today. Thank You that the Blood of Jesus protects us from the destroyer. May the Blood of Jesus remain constantly on the doorposts of our lives, Amen.

Day 14

OPENING PRAYER

*D*ear God, thank You for a cheerful spirit! Because I know that You make all things work for good for those who love You, I rejoice, confident in the things You are doing for me. Though whatever the enemy throws at me is meant for evil, I know that You mean it for my good, and I have received that good today. In the name of Jesus, Amen.

LESSON: MOSES AND JOSHUA

The Israelites were God's chosen people. As the descendants of Abraham, they had the same relationship to God and the very same Covenant with God that Abraham did.

Take heart! We are God's chosen people as well. Instead of Moses, we have the Holy Spirit to guide us.

Soak in the truth of that today.

God chose to send His Son to die for your sins; you are a "blessed one," just like Abraham.

Now we return to our friends, the Israelites, in the wilderness of Sinai. They whined about not having any water or food so God sent them sweet water and manna. God took Moses up to Mount Sinai, where He gave him *"...all the rules and regulations*" (Exodus 24:3). All the Israelites told Moses in "*...unison: 'Everything God said, we'll do'.*"

Read and highlight Exodus 24:4-8. Record what Moses said after he sprinkled the blood over the people.

Moses then returned to Mount Sinai for 40 days and 40 nights. Exodus chapters 25-31 outline in detail God's directives for how the Israelites should worship Him. Write down what happened in Exodus 31:18.

While Moses was on Mount Sinai, the people got restless. Aaron made a golden calf that they worshipped and God became *angry*. Read and highlight Exodus 32:7-14. Record anything that stands out to you.

Now read and highlight Exodus 33:11-23. My favorite verses are 11, 14 and 17. I find a great deal of comfort in these verses. Write an overview of them here:

God is a God of detail. He takes time and goes to great lengths to explain covenant conditions, sacrificial procedures and commandments. I would encourage you to read Exodus, Leviticus, Numbers, and Deuteronomy in their entirety and highlight everything that jumps out at you. Moses wrote all of these books. Moses was there. God spoke to Moses, in fact, God communicated to the Israelites exclusively through Moses and Aaron.

Let us move on now to the book of Numbers, which includes a lot of bickering, questioning and rebelling against God and Moses. Although Moses was humble, the constant complaining of the Israelites took a toll on him. Read and highlight Numbers

14:19-30. Whom did God say would make it to the Promised Land?

How did Caleb "follow" God?

Read and highlight Numbers 20:6-12. Why are Aaron and Moses unable to lead the people into the Promised Land (Verse 12)?

We will conclude our study of the legacy of Moses with the book of Deuteronomy.

Moses gave his final message to the Israelites in the Plains of Moab before he died and before they crossed over into the Promised Land. (This was the longest sermon recorded in the Bible.) Moses wanted to make sure that the Israelites remembered every detail of their experience in the wilderness; also reiterating the laws and commandments that the Israelites would follow when they entered the Promised Land. Finally, he blessed them.

Read and highlight Deuteronomy 31:14-15.

God commissioned Joshua to take the lead after Moses died. Record what God told Joshua in Deuteronomy 31:23.

God knew that Joshua had a difficult task ahead of him. He encouraged Joshua and reassured him that He would be with him. I am sure that Joshua needed to hear those words from God. He had seen how rebellious these people were in spite of all God had done for them. I am sure Joshua realized that this task was going to be difficult.

Let us end this session by thanking God for encouraging us when the task seems too large. Thank God for being with you and for guiding you as you take on the extraordinary task that He has planned for you. Know today that God is telling you *"Be strong. Take Courage!"*

MEMORIZATION

Did you know the Prophets we have memorized so far are called the "Major" Prophets and the rest are known as the "Minor" Prophets? For today, just review the ones you have so far.

PRAYER OF AGREEMENT

Lord, thank You for Your Word today. Seal it in our hearts, and show us the application of it in our everyday lives, that like Joshua we will be strong and courageous, Amen.

Day 15

OPENING PRAYER

I love Your Word, Lord. I place it above all other things in my life. I spend more quality time learning about Your testimonies and directives than anything else. I think about them all day long and meditate on them. I delight in Your statutes and in Your ways, and I write them on the tablet of my heart. Make my life a picture of Your Word. Amen.

LESSON: REVIEW

Our lesson today will be more of a review; instead of learning new material we will go over our past lessons and commit them to memory.

LESSON EXERCISES

What did we learn about God through Abraham?

What did we learn about God through Isaac?

What did we learn about God through Jacob?

What about Joseph?

What about Moses?

Finally, what did we learn about God through Joshua?

What kind of an impact do these men have on us today?

What can you apply from their teaching that will help to shape the legacy you will leave?

MEMORIZATION

Today, add Hosea and Joel to your Books of the Prophets card, and review all books so far.

PRAYER OF AGREEMENT

Lord, we lift up our Bible Study partner before You, and we ask that You would be with them today through all their struggles and challenges, and we thank You that they have the victory in every area of their life, In Jesus' name, Amen.

Day 16

OPENING PRAYER

Cleanse me this day from all selfish desires, O Lord! Create in me a clean heart, a heart that desires only those things You desire for me Lord. I cry out to be made more like You in every way and to minister to others the things You would want me to minister to them. In Christ's name, Amen.

LESSON: JOSHUA

We will now meet an ordinary man who sought and knew an extraordinary God. Joshua was with Moses from the very beginning of the exodus from Egypt. He took part in every event and was the military commander in the first battle that the Israelites faced upon leaving Egypt. He had been Moses' personal assistant since his youth. Now he would be Moses' successor.

He would be leading the Israelites into the land flowing with milk and honey that had been promised to Abraham almost 500 years earlier. Joshua knew the presence and the power of God.

Read and highlight Joshua 1:1-9.

Do you remember God's words to Abraham in Genesis 13:17? He told Abraham, *"Get moving"...* and now he is telling Joshua *"Get going."*

God told Joshua he was close now; the land was just past the Jordan River. *"It is all yours. All your life, no one will be able to hold out against you. In the same way I was with Moses, I'll be with you. I won't give up on you; I won't leave you. Strength! Courage! You are going to lead this people to inherit the land that I promised to give their ancestors. Give it everything you have, heart and soul."* Joshua heard God and he knew God would do everything He said.

Joshua sent two spies to scout out Jericho. They stayed with a prostitute named Rahab, and she willingly assisted the spies. Read and highlight Joshua 2:8-11 and record why Rahab was so willing to help the spies:

The people in her "country" had heard all about God's plan to give the land in which she lived to the Israelites. They had probably heard it for the last 500 years like the Israelites had. Rahab believed everything she had heard about how God delivered the Israelites from Egypt. Read and highlight Joshua 2:12-14. What did she ask in return?

The spies reported to Joshua, *"Yes! God has given the whole country to us. Everybody there is in a state of panic because of us."*

Read and highlight Joshua 3:1-17. What took place in these verses? Do you see a parallel between the beginning of the journey and the end of the journey? If so, what is the parallel?

Once again, God completely opens a body of water and the Israelites are able to walk across on dry ground. After the

Israelites were across the Jordan, God tells Joshua to get 12 stones from the middle of the Jordan.

Read and highlight Joshua 4:1-7. God wants to make sure the legacy of faith continues. How wonderful it will be for the Israelites to show the stones taken from the Jordan and tell their children about their final journey to the Promised Land. Before the Israelites proceeded, each male had to be circumcised in order to demonstrate their sanctification to God's service. Remember the original covenant of circumcision made with Abraham. This act would demonstrate that the Israelites were indeed the sons of Abraham and would be bound to serve God as he did.

It is no coincidence that Israel got to Jericho just in time to celebrate the Passover. This generation of Israelites had never celebrated the Passover. In fact, the Israelites did not celebrate the Passover for nearly 39 years due to the disobedience of the original Israelites at the border of Canaan, where they were condemned to die before reaching the Promised Land.

What a great opportunity for Joshua to discuss the events that led up to the glorious time in which they were living. What a privilege they must have felt to be the ones chosen to enter into the land promised to Abraham, Isaac and Jacob. After the Passover celebration, the manna stopped. The people were now able to eat food grown in the land they had been promised.

Read and highlight Joshua 6:1-5. Everything happened just as God had instructed. Now, read and highlight Joshua 6:22-25.

The Israelites spared Rahab as promised. Can you imagine being Rahab? She might have felt undeserving, yet God saved her because she believed. She also hid the spies when they first scouted out Jericho, and she helped them escape. In addition to this, Rahab is in the direct bloodline of Jesus!

Joshua continued to be diligent in seeking and following God in everything he did until the entire land was conquered. In Joshua's last address to the Israelites, he commanded them to *"stay strong and steady."* He told them to be obedient to God's covenant laws and reminded them to love and follow God. In his final act as God's servant, Joshua renewed the covenant agreement originally made with Abraham. He then recited all that the people had been through and reminded them that God had been with them and had been their guide the entire time. Joshua went on to explain that it was their choice who to follow. Write what he said in Joshua 24:15.

What about you? Whom will you follow? Recite that scripture to our Heavenly Father.

MEMORIZATION

Review all the books you have memorized so far. Now add Amos and Obadiah to your Prophets list.

PRAYER OF AGREEMENT

Father, send a Rahab into my reader's life and my life to help us complete our missions. We thank You for placing the right people ahead of us to assist us on our journeys. In Jesus' name, Amen.

Day 17

OPENING PRAYER

Father, I receive Your favor today. As I begin my Bible Study and as I go through my day, please help me to do those things that activate Your favor, and behave in such a way that the favor flows in my life. I ask also that You would give me favor with those You bring across my path, and open doors that no man can shut. Amen.

LESSON: RUTH

I had not originally intended to include Ruth in this study, but as I began to study David, I learned that Ruth was King David's great grandmother and was an extraordinary woman. I enjoyed learning about her and I think you will as well.

The book of Ruth is one of two books in the Bible named after a woman. We have become used to reading and highlighting passages about mighty men, who made a significant impact, but the Book of Ruth is different; it focuses on an insignificant woman who was not even born an Israelite.

Ruth was a Moabite.

(Bear with me on this as I give you a quick history on the Moabites.)

Abraham's nephew, Lot, had two daughters who got him drunk and had sex with him because they wanted to carry on the family name. They both got pregnant and the older daughter had a son and named him Moab. He later became the father of the Moabites. The younger daughter had a son and named him Ben Ammi and he became the father of the Ammonites. Both nations became enemies of Abraham's descendants.

Now, Ruth was married to Mahlon, an Israelite who had moved to Moab during a famine. Ruth's father-in-law died, leaving her mother-in-law, Naomi, alone. Ten years later Mahlon and his brother died as well. Naomi was grief stricken.

Naomi had heard news that God had shown favor to Bethlehem and blessed them with crops, so she and both her daughters-in-law packed their things and began a journey to Bethlehem. Naomi asked the daughters-in-law to return to Moab to be with their families because she had nothing to offer them. Opah, (one of the daughters-in-law) decided to return to her home. Read and highlight Ruth 1:16-22. What does Ruth decide?

Ruth demonstrated her loyalty, love and devotion to Naomi by proclaiming that Naomi's God and people would be her own. In Bethlehem, Ruth began her new life taking care of Naomi by gleaning from the barley harvest. She gleaned in a field owned by a man named Boaz, a relative of one of her late fathers-in-law.

Boaz was a man of God who had great compassion for his workers. He was in the field one day telling his workers, "God be with you," when he saw Ruth and asked his supervisor who she was. The supervisor informed Boaz that she had returned from Moab with Naomi and had asked if she could "glean" from the field. He went on to tell him that she had been hard at work without a break since early that morning. Read and highlight Ruth 2:8-23 and summarize what takes place.

Continue to read and highlight this beautiful and enchanting story in Ruth Chapters 3 and 4. Summarize the events in your Journal.

In this story, God showed favor to Ruth, allowed her to enter new fellowship with the Israelites, and sealed the covenant with her marriage to Boaz. Ruth, therefore, became part of David's lineage and ultimately our Saviors lineage. How amazing is God? The entire Old Testament is devoted to God's provision for His people. The book of Ruth further demonstrates the beginning of God's expansion and inclusion of foreigners into His "chosen people." He was paving the way for us to be able to leave a legacy of faith in Him rather than a hopeless life without Him.

Please take time today to thank God for including us as His chosen people.

MEMORIZATION

Today, include Jonah and Micah on your Prophets card. There are only six more Old Testament Books to add to your list before we move on to the New Testament Books. Do not forget to review all the names of the books you have memorized so far!

PRAYER OF AGREEMENT

Lord, send a Boaz into my reader's and my life as we need them. At those times when it appears that we must glean in the fields, send someone who will provide the resources we need to fulfill Your assignments. In Jesus' name, Amen.

Day 18

OPENING PRAYER

*L*ord, *as I begin my Bible Study today, help me to always choose Your best for me, and to wait for Your best instead of choosing something less because of impatience or because it looks good or looks right for me. I receive Your goodness and Your best for me today, in the name of Jesus, Amen.*

LESSON: SAUL AND DAVID (PART 1)

Saul was the first anointed king of Israel. Saul was a courageous and generous leader in the beginning. He disobeyed the word of God on several occasions though, which finally resulted in Samuel, the prophet, informing Saul that because he rejected God's command, God would reject him as King.

In 1 Samuel 16 we find God instructing Samuel on who the next King would be. He told Samuel to go to Bethlehem and look for the sons of Jesse (Refer to Ruth 4:18-22).

Read and highlight 1 Samuel 16:6-13. At first, whom did Samuel think God meant to anoint? Do you remember when we talked about how God chooses leaders? What does that tell you about how He chooses a king? Even when others see us as runts, God looks at our hearts and says, "This is the one!"

63

Let us pause a moment and whisper a prayer of thanksgiving: *Thank you most gracious Heavenly Father for viewing me differently than the world views me. Amen.*

David went through a great deal before he became King. David conquered Goliath and Saul became jealous. Then Saul realized God was with David and Saul's jealousy turned to hatred. Saul plotted to kill David, but his son Jonathan stepped in and reminded him that David had done nothing wrong. Saul listened to Jonathan and said, *"You're right. As God lives, David lives. He will not be killed."*

One day David was playing his harp for Saul and a *"black mood from God settled on Saul."* Saul took his spear and tried to kill David but he missed. David ran to Samuel and told him everything that Saul had done. David then went to Jonathan, Saul's son, with whom he had developed a strong friendship. Jonathan vowed to keep David informed of Saul's actions, but Saul knew that Jonathan and David were best friends and he became so angry that he even tried to kill Jonathan. Finally, Jonathan realized his father was serious about killing David, so he sent David away.

Read and highlight 1 Samuel 22:1-2.

I find it funny that 400 *"losers and vagrants and misfits"* came to David and he became their leader. They must have known David had a heart for them. He understood them; after all, he had been a runt himself!

Therefore, this motley crew led by David set out to hide in the Desert. Saul and his army looked for David day after day, but God never allowed them to find him. David actively sought God during this time. In 1 Samuel 22:1-6, David sought God's guidance. Once again, in 1 Samuel 23:9-12 David sought God's guidance. David knew his leader. He knew that he could do anything with God on his side; all he had to do was ask and God was quick to respond.

David's men grew in number and kept moving and Saul continued to pursue David. Read and highlight 1 Samuel 24. Summarize the events that took place. Why did David spare Saul?

David behaved wisely in every way. David chose his words wisely. He was not going to fight evil with evil. Instead, he was going to allow God to be the Judge. God knew David's heart. He knew that David would call on His name when he was in need and God knew that David would follow His direction. God had confidence in David. Can you say the same? Where is your heart? Are you seeking God? Are you allowing Him to answer before you go any further?

Pray today that you would have the courage to be a modern-day David, seeking God; especially when you are running from demons in the desert. We will return to the adventures of David tomorrow!

LESSON EXERCISES

Look again at 2 Samuel 23:8-39. Some of David's misfits became some of the mightiest warriors in the Bible. Can you name some of them from the text?

MEMORIZATION

Today, add Nahum and Habakkuk to your Prophets card. There are many prophets!

PRAYER OF AGREEMENT

Heavenly Father, make my reader and me people after your own heart, as David was. Anoint us to carry out Your will and grant us strength and patience for the journey. In the name of Jesus I pray, Amen.

Day 19

OPENING PRAYER

*H*eavenly Father, I thank You for deliverance today from all the tricks of the enemy. As I study Your Word please show me all the ways in which I must resist the enemy. Lord, I submit to You and to Your will, and I set myself to walk in all Your ways. Amen.

LESSON: DAVID (PART2)

We ended our scripture reading yesterday with Saul thanking David for sparing his life. Saul had temporary remorse for his actions against David, but quickly went back to his desire to kill him. In 1 Samuel 26, Saul was told where David was hiding and he quickly gathered 3,000 men to continue their search.

David learned that Saul was near and was once again in pursuit. David set out with one of his military leaders, Abishai, to scout out Saul's camp. They were able to walk right into Saul's camp while Saul and his men were sleeping without waking anyone. Abishai was ready to kill Saul immediately. David showed respect for God's anointed and told Abishai not to kill Saul, but to take Saul's spear and water jug, which were next to his head.

Read and highlight 1 Samuel 26:13-25. Saul attempted once again to show remorse, but David knew he would still try to kill him again so he and his men escaped to Gath, and Saul finally called off the hunt.

David and his men settled down with Achish, son of the King of Gath, who ruled over the Philistine country. Achish was impressed with David and allowed him and his men to settle at Ziklag. When the Philistines declared war on Israel, Achish told David that he and his men could march with his troops. Record David's response to Achish in 1 Samuel 28:2.

David continued to be bold. He knew where his strength came from and Achish believed David. However, the Philistine officers were suspicious of David and his men. The officers told Achish to send David back to Ziklag. Read and highlight 1 Samuel 29:6-11.

In reality, this freed David from a dilemma. He would have had to fight against his own country with men he knew were enemies of God's chosen people. Achish admired David and even called him God's angel. However, Achish knew he had to honor the wishes of the Philistine officers.

David and his men returned to Ziklag only to find it burned to the ground and all of the families taken prisoner by the Amalekites. David's men were so upset they considered stoning David.

Imagine that, just when David thought things could not get any worse, they did. Who does David turn to in his time of distress? Read and highlight 1 Samuel 30: 6-7 and record the answer.

I find David to be truly amazing. Have you ever been in a situation where you thought you could not go any further?

Many times in the past when I found myself in this situation, I did not turn to God, as I should have. I would convince myself that I deserved my plight and that God would rescue me when He was ready. I would lean on my own understanding and then find the pit I was in getting larger and larger.

It used to take me a while to lean on God. In fact, I tended to turn to people first. I learned to lean on God after reading Bible stories about men like David, who knew beyond any doubt that God was in control. They turned to Him believing that He would give the answers and I saw repeatedly that God did answer them when they sought Him.

Are you seeking God for answers? Are you turning to Him in your time of need? What need do you have right now? List your needs and seek God for the answer.

God answered David and instructed him to "go after" the Amalekites. David and his men pursued their raiders, rescued their people, and took back all that was theirs just as God had said. Upon returning to Ziklag David learned that Saul and his three sons died in the war waged by the Philistines. Even after everything Saul had done to him, David mourned his death. David was especially mournful for the loss of his friend Jonathan. Read, highlight and record what he wrote in his song of lament in 2 Samuel 1:26.

David was everything that we should strive to be. He was a man after God's heart, he was a mighty warrior, a leader, a forgiver and he was an amazing friend. Take time now to thank God for David's example.

MEMORIZATION

There are only four more Old Testament Books to go! Review all the names of the books you have and then add Zephaniah and Haggai.

PRAYER OF AGREEMENT

Lord, as my reader and I go through rough times, even when it seems some are out to do us harm, place a special hedge of protection around us, and assign Your guardian angels watch over us. Thank You for this in the mighty name of Jesus, Amen.

Day 20

OPENING PRAYER

*L*ord, give me a heart of obedience — daily, hourly obedience. *Let me never stray from keeping Your Word and doing all You tell me to do. I set myself to please You, and I make that my greatest goal each and every day from now on. I thank You that You have set me on a right and correct path, and I trust that You are directing all my steps. In Jesus' name, Amen.*

LESSON: DAVID (PART 3)

Saul died, and David, at the age of 30, became King over Israel.

Please read and highlight 2 Samuel 7 (The same story is covered in 1 Chronicles 17).

King David's heart was full of gratitude toward God. He told his prophet Nathan he felt guilty about living in a comfortable home and leaving the Chest of God (Ark of the Covenant) in a tent. However, that night God gave Nathan a covenant promise to convey to His servant David. God told Nathan that David would not build a house for the Chest of God. Instead, King David's job would be to secure peace throughout Israel. God promoted him from shepherding a herd of sheep to shepherding His chosen people.

God gave Nathan a wonderful play on David's words. He said that David is not to build God a house or a temple; instead, God is going to build David a royal dynasty. It was a house that stood for many years to come.

God had been building Israel since the days of Abraham. Now He told David that his legacy of faith would continue through the rule of one of his own children. That child would be the one to "build a house" to honor God. God went on to say that David's house and kingdom would establish rule permanently. In this statement, God was laying the foundational covenant promise of the coming of Jesus Christ, who was in the direct lineage of David and whose reign would endure forever. God's covenant promise to David is the very provision we live under today.

Copy King David's prayer in 2 Samuel 7:21-29 word for word in your Journal.

King David acknowledged that what God was saying not only affected that immediate generation, but many, many generations to follow. King David, humbled by God, laid claim to His promise.

Is there a promise God has whispered to you? Has He promised you good health or a Godly mate? Has He provided you with a glimpse of the future? If He has, lay claim to it just like King David did. Ask Him to "guarantee it permanently" and to "Do exactly" what He has promised. It is time to be bold in our prayers. God loves that. He wants us to believe Him and His word. Ask Him to give you a glimpse of your future so that you may lay claim to His promise for you personally. Record your prayers and promises in your Journal.

MEMORIZATION

Add Zachariah and Malachi to your list of Prophets, and with those two you are done with your Prophets card, and you are done with your Books of the Old Testament. Well done!

PRAYER OF AGREEMENT

Lord, grant my reader and me comfort and joy in our times of disappointment. May Romans 8:28 be made real to us every day, knowing that You ARE making all things work to the good for those who love You! Amen.

Day 21

OPENING PRAYER

Dear Father, I am desperate for You today. I desire a closer walk with You and have a greater understanding of those things You want me to know. I tie myself to You today and I set myself to continue in all that You would have me do. In the name of Jesus, Amen.

LESSON: DAVID (PART 4)

David was a man after God's heart, but he was not perfect.

Read and highlight 2 Samuel 11:2-5. Record the events in your Journal.

I find myself wanting to narrate this like a reality television show, but I will spare you... this time. David got himself into a real mess. He saw Bathsheba in all her beauty and decided he wanted to have his way with her. There was just one problem. Bathsheba was married, and she was not married to just anyone. She was married to one of David's mighty men; a warrior named Uriah who had been fighting in the war. David pursued her anyway and got her pregnant. David then attempted to get Uriah drunk so he would go home and sleep with Bathsheba and he would think the baby was his.

Uriah, however, was loyal to his call of duty and did not go home, so David sent Uriah back to the front lines of the war so that he would die and David could marry Bathsheba as quickly as possible. Uriah died and after her time of mourning was over, (around seven days) David married her.

Not only did David violate four of the Ten Commandments, he blatantly abused the royal power that God entrusted to him.

God sent Nathan the prophet to rebuke David. Nathan confronted David and told him a parable to humble him.

Read and highlight 2 Samuel 12:1-25.

After Nathan got the reaction from David that he was seeking, he told David, *"You're the man."* Not only did he tell David that he was the man, but he went on to point out all God had done for David. In verse 11, God promised David *"murder and killing will continually plague your family."* He told David that what David had done in private, God will do in public. David confessed that he had sinned against God and God forgave David.

However, God further punished David by taking away the son that Bathsheba was carrying. God did what He said He would. David's son died on the seventh day. Upon learning of his child's death, David cleaned up, changed clothes and went to worship. By going to God and worshipping, David demonstrated his humble acceptance of God's discipline.

God blessed Bathsheba and David with another son, and they named him Solomon. God showed favor and love for Solomon and named him Jedidiah; meaning "God's Beloved". David's name also meant "Beloved of God." The two names having the same meaning signified that Solomon would be God's choice of David's successor to the throne.

God fulfilled His promise to David that *"murder and killing will continually plague your family."* It all began when Amnon, David's son, fell in love with his half-sister, Tamar, whose brother was Absalom. Amnon was so obsessed with Tamar that he raped her. Absalom found out about the rape and eventually killed Amnon. Absalom went on to become popular with the people and had an enormous following. Swelled with pride and believing he deserved the throne, he declared war on his father, King David. David organized his troops to fight and ordered them to *"deal gently"* with Absalom. In the end, Absalom dies, and King David was devastated.

Read and highlight 1 Kings Chapter 1.

Here we find King David advanced in years to the point where he must name his successor. His son Abonijah, who had never been disciplined and was *"spoiled rotten,"* decided on his own that he was going to be the "next king." Upon hearing Abonijah's plan, Nathan the prophet warned Bathsheba, who immediately went to King David. The King told Bathsheba that he would follow through with his promise and would make Solomon king that very day.

When Abonijah heard that King David named Solomon king, Abonijah went to the new king and begged not to be killed. Solomon said he would not harm him, *"If he proves to be a man of honor"*... *"but if there is evil in him, he'll die."*

Abonijah could not let it rest. Solomon was forced to order his death because he requested permission to marry a woman who was considered part of David's harem. This action signified another attempt on Abonijah's part to claim the throne.

Read and highlight 1 Chronicles 22:1-19.

God told David through Nathan the prophet, that he would not be the one to build The Temple to honor God. It would be David's son instead.

Summarize what David said in 1 Chronicles 22:11-16 in your Journal.

Thank God for David's legacy and teaching. He did as God instructed and then passed the formula for success on to Solomon. This formula still works today. If we follow the direction of God and do as He instructs and commands, then we will be successful!

LESSON EXERCISES

David's last words were very powerful. List as many ways as you can how those words apply in your personal life today.

MEMORIZATION

Review the names of all Old Testament Books. If you have fallen behind this is a great time to catch up!

PRAYER OF AGREEMENT

Heavenly Father, thank You for Your forgiving heart. When my reader or I are found in a fault or in sin, restore us with Your loving kindness, and show us Your mercy and love. Keep us ever mindful that we are Your children and the Blood of Your Son cleanses us. In His name, Amen.

Day 22

OPENING PRAYER

Heavenly Father, I lay my entire life before You. I hold nothing back. Every thought, every desire, every idea, and everything I am, I expose to You for examination. Take away those things You hate from my life, even if it hurts; cut away those rotten parts that have no life and none of Your character. Strengthen those things that reflect who You are, and who You want me to be. Make me Your chosen vessel! In Jesus' name, Amen.

LESSON: DAVID AND SOLOMON

David was close to dying and he anointed his son, Solomon, to be King of all Israel and Judah. He also informed Solomon he would be the one to build The Temple. David bought the supplies, but Solomon would be the one to build it. After David gave Solomon orders to build The Temple, David began to "sort" the leaders into "work groups." I think it is interesting that David gave specific instructions about the music, security guards, finances, military, administrators, suppliers and counselors for his son. He wanted to make sure he covered every detail before his death. David then gives public instruction to Solomon.

Read and highlight 1 Chronicles 28:9-10.

David knew that God examined the heart. After all, David was himself a man after God's own heart. Do you remember the words *"If you seek him, he'll make sure you find him"*? David went on to give Solomon *"the plans for The Temple complex."* I love the way The Message translation says David, *"turned over the plans for everything that God's Spirit had brought to his mind."*

Did you know you have God's Spirit inside of you ready and waiting for you to map out the plans that He brings to your mind? In David's time God's Spirit only dwelled in His priests, prophets and leaders. Today, because of Jesus, all Christians have the ability to tap into that same Spirit that instructed David.

What is God's Spirit, otherwise known to us as the Holy Spirit, saying to you? Is He giving you the blueprints for something? Maybe He is prompting you to change your lifestyle or change your job. Maybe He is asking for your full commitment to Him and is calling you to be an amazing man or woman of faith. Whatever the prompting, listen and be obedient to the call. He loves you, will be with you, and will guide you.

Find comfort in the words that David spoke in 1 Chronicles 28:20-21. Record them in your Journal as if he was speaking these words directly to you.

"Take charge! Take Heart! Don't be anxious or get discouraged. God, my God, is with you in this; He won't walk off and leave you in a lurch."

Do you believe that?

Stop for a moment and thank God for placing the same Spirit in us, which He gave David. Ask the Lord to forgive us for not tapping into His Spirit. Ask Him to help us not be anxious, but to be courageous as we do His will.

Finally, King David died. He was close to 70 years old having lived a good life full of honor and wealth.

King Solomon hit the floor running and God was with Him.

Read and highlight 2 Chronicles 1:7-12 and record in your Journal what took place.

I think most of us are familiar with this scripture. God could have given Solomon anything, riches, glory, honor, but he asked for *wisdom and knowledge*. God's response demonstrated how pleased He was with Solomon's request. He not only granted Solomon wisdom and knowledge, He presented *"the rest as a bonus - money, wealth, and fame beyond anything the kings before or after you had or will have."* Only God is capable of providing these things. He loved and showed favor to Solomon from his birth.

Solomon quickly got a reputation for being the wisest man in the land. During his reign as king there was peace across the entire country. People from surrounding nations and faraway lands came to hear his teaching.

Read, highlight and summarize 1 Kings 4:29-34.

The account of Solomon's work on The Temple is recorded in 1 Kings Chapters 5-8 and 2 Chronicles chapters 2-7. Let us focus our attention on 2 Chronicles 2-7.

The Temple construction took approximately 20 years. Thousands of men assisted in this monumental task. King Hiram of Tyre collaborated with Solomon by providing the cedar, cypress and algum logs. He also sent him a "master artisan" who supervised Solomon's trained staff.

Read and highlight King Hiram's response to Solomon's request in 2 Chronicles 2:11-16. Record some of the precious words that he wrote.

Construction on The Temple began in the fourth year of Solomon's reign. God instructed him to build The Temple on Mount Moriah in Jerusalem. This location holds major biblical significance. Abraham nearly sacrificed Isaac on the very same mountain. Mount Moriah would also be the location of countless animal ritual offerings in The Temple. These sacrifices would lead to the ultimate sacrifice of God's Lamb, Jesus Christ, in the same location on Mount Moriah.

I hope you are beginning to recognize the thread that God has woven from one generation to another. God does nothing by chance. There is a perfect plan that we can trace through the Bible if we take the time. His Word and His works are amazing. I love the foreshadowing that leads to the ultimate atonement of our sins, the sacrifice of Jesus, our Savior and King. Who am I to receive this precious gift from God? Do you understand the magnitude of God's love for you as laid out in the Bible? Please take your Journal and write a prayer of appreciation to God for His perfect plan.

MEMORIZATION

Review the names of all Old Testament Books. Is it beginning to get easier?

PRAYER OF AGREEMENT

Lord, give my reader and me wisdom and understanding. Grant us comprehension of Your Word, insight into Your thoughts and intentions, prudence to see the path before us, and skill in everything You have called us to do. In the name of Jesus, Amen.

Day 23

OPENING PRAYER

Lord, I spend time with You right now, today in the name of Jesus. I repent of all those times when You longed to share Yourself with me, and I decided to spend that time on other things or on myself instead. I desire to know You in a deeper and more intimate way. Bare Your own heart to me now Lord. I want to know You more. Amen.

LESSON: KING SOLOMON

After completing The Temple, Solomon experienced some serious problems. King Solomon had obtained respect all over the region. Some scholars believe that because of that respect he was able to do business with foreign dignitaries who felt compelled to return his generosity by providing him with wives and concubines. In fact, Solomon had 700 royal wives and 300 concubines. It is fair to say that King Solomon was a ladies' man.

The Bible describes him as *"obsessed with women."* Can you imagine what his house must have been like? The problem - other than the obvious - is that the surrounding nations worshipped pagan gods. This was a direct violation of God's teaching.

Read and highlight Exodus 34:13-16. God warned the people if they marry women who worship pagan gods they themselves would end up *"doing the same thing."* Solomon had an *"obsession for women"* and *"openly defied God."* Record what took place in 1 Kings 11:6-13 in your journal.

How in the world can this man go from being the wisest of all kings to making God *"furious"* because of his abandonment and disobedience? Actually, it is not that hard. Fame, fortune and an insatiable appetite for things that do not honor God will do it every time!

Let us take a moment to examine how this could happen in our own lives. When we put God first, amazing things happen. We have peace, even amidst the storms of life. We have joy through all circumstances and we are able to accomplish things we could never have done on our own. However, the minute we get prideful, arrogant or comfortable and step out of God's will, things start to change. If we do not repent, things go on changing – for the worse.

This process takes time. Our disobedience and its effects usually do not happen overnight. It happens slowly. Perhaps we begin to accept things we would not have accepted before; a TV show, music, bad language. Perhaps we do things we would not have done while seeking God's will.

God will go to great measures to bring us back to obedience. He will discipline us because He cares for us. He is our parent, our daddy God. He loves us and wants us to avoid the things that continually hurt us. It is our choice whether or not we go back. How many times do we have to get hurt before we learn that it is not worth it?

I lived a life of disobedience for years. I suffered from pride, arrogance, and self-righteousness. I chose to continue these behaviors. Then God took away the very thing that made me feel most comfortable. It took time, but in my state of brokenness and desperation, I ended up seeking Him. Just as His Word says, He was there waiting, willing to instruct and direct me in His ways. It brings tears to my eyes to think of the parallel between my life of disobedience and King Solomon's.

I still struggle with pride, arrogance and self-righteousness. Thank the Lord who gives us His Word as a reminder. I needed the example of Solomon in my life to help me realize that I am no better than he is. I may not have 700 pagan husbands, but my disobedience is just as dangerous and can separate me from my Heavenly Father just as much.

God disciplined Solomon by provoking his adversaries. He also took away all of the tribes of Israel, excluding one, Judah. Finally, God said that He would respect His servant David by not taking the kingdom away from Solomon. He said, *"It's your son who will pay-I'll rip it out of his grasp."*

We have seen repeatedly that God is a God of His Word. God grants Jeroboam, a man who served in Solomon's administration, the Ten Tribes.

Read, highlight and record the instructions that God gave to Jeroboam in 1 Kings 11:37-39.

Before Solomon's death, he tried to kill Jeroboam. The reason for Solomon's attempt on Jeroboam's life is not clear. Perhaps he discovered that God had given Jeroboam the Ten

Tribes. Regardless, Solomon died and was buried in the city of David and his son Rehoboam succeeded him as king of Judah.

LESSON EXERCISES

Between the time of Solomon and the time of the captivity of Babylon, there were many Kings of Judah and of Israel. Can you name some of them?

MEMORIZATION

Review the names of all Old Testament Books. Tomorrow we will begin the New Testament, so have your next index card ready to go!

PRAYER OF AGREEMENT

Heavenly Father, "God of restoration," fully restore my reader and me including all that the enemy has ever taken from us. Make all our paths straight before us. In Jesus' name, Amen.

Day 24

OPENING PRAYER

*L*ord, *let Your light shine through my life today. I long to be a light in the dark world. May I show Your loving kindness to all. In the name of Jesus I pray, Amen.*

LESSON: EZRA

Ezra was a priest, a man of strong conviction who believed God was with the Israelites. He was a model of the legacy we should strive to leave behind. He was a man of love and devotion to the Lord and in return, God was with Him. In fact, the name Ezra means, *"The Lord helps."*

By this time in history, the Israelites had been through a great deal. They had been a rebellious nation and because of their rebellion, the nation split after the fall of King Solomon. After many Kings ruled Israel and many other kings ruled Judah, God had enough and allowed Babylon to rule over all Israel. This all changed 70 years later.

Cyrus, king of Persia, captured Babylon and took over as king. This fulfilled a prophecy by Jeremiah that the Babylonians would hold the Israelites in captivity for 70 years. (Read and highlight Jeremiah 25:11-12) In the 70th year of their captivity, the king of Persia took over and the Lord prompted him to build another Temple for God in Jerusalem.

Record what King Cyrus wrote in his announcement to the people in Ezra 1:1-4.

What a breath of fresh air this must have been for the Israelites. They were going back to their hometown where they would be able to worship the way God had instructed Moses. King Cyrus even gave them back the Temple articles King Nebuchadnezzar took during his plunder of the original Temple of God.

As they poured the foundation for the new Temple, they worshipped God by making burnt offerings. In the tradition of the former king of Israel, David, they sang praises to God. They said *"Yes! God is good! Oh yes – He'll never quit loving Israel!"* At the dedication of The Temple, the Israelites sacrificed bulls, rams and goats. "... *-And as an Absolution-Offering for all Israel, twelve he-goats, one for each of the twelve tribes of Israel."* They placed the priests in their divisions and the Levites in their places for the service of God in Jerusalem – all as was written in the Book of Moses.

It was time for the next Exodus of Israel – back to Jerusalem. The king of Persia appointed Ezra to lead the Israelites out of Babylon to Jerusalem. I want you to read and highlight Ezra 7:27-28; Ezra 8:15-36; Ezra 9 and Ezra 10:1-17. Also, Nehemiah Chapter 8 and 9:1-3. You are going to love reading about this man and his dedication to the Lord.

LESSON EXERCISES

What were some of the most significant events of the Exodus of the Israelites back to Israel from Babylon?

MEMORIZATION

Today is the day we begin memorizing the names of the books of the New Testament! After reviewing your Old Testament Books, begin your new index card by writing Gospels at the top, and writing 1-5 on the left hand side. Then write the names of the Gospels: Matthew, Mark, Luke and John, and add Acts as well. (The book of Acts is not a Gospel, but since it is a continuation or sequel of the Gospel of Luke, we are including it here).

PRAYER OF AGREEMENT

Lord, according to Your Word equip my reader and myself with every provision, resource, talent, and gift necessary for us to fulfill Your will. In the name of Jesus, Amen.

Day 25

OPENING PRAYER

*D**ear Heavenly Father, fill me today. Let me see and recognize and know You like I have never known You before. My heart longs to know You deeper. Amen.*

LESSON: NEHEMIAH

We left our friends, the Israelites, in the hands of Ezra appointed by the king of Persia, to lead the Israelites out of Babylon to Jerusalem. We learned that Ezra, the priest, sought God and believed wholeheartedly what God had to say. God protected Ezra and the Jews on their journey back to Jerusalem.

Now we move on to one of my favorite books and stories of the Bible. Nehemiah was a cupbearer for King Artaxerxes. Nehemiah discovered that the Jews who had arrived in Jerusalem were in *"…bad shape."* Nehemiah was another example of a man who sought after God. After learning the conditions in Jerusalem were deplorable, Nehemiah felt burdened and began to fast and pray before God.

Please read and highlight Nehemiah 1:4-11 and record what he prayed in your Journal.

Nehemiah knew God was faithful. He also knew that God's people had been terrible to Him. He prayed *"day and night in intercession"* for the people of Israel. He knew that his status with the King would assist him in his endeavor to revitalize Jerusalem. The king granted his desire to rebuild the wall around Jerusalem and he appointed Nehemiah Governor.

Before we go on, I want you to think about what Nehemiah did when he learned about the conditions in Israel. He prayed and fasted for days. When we have burdens on our heart and we are confused, we can pray and fast like Nehemiah. One of my favorite things to do is intercede on others behalf. We are to seek God to assist our fellow Christians in times of need. What an honor it is to stand in the gap for others and allow God to use us as he did Nehemiah.

Nehemiah was not being arrogant. He did not desire the position of Governor; he just had a deep longing for his fellow Jews to have their city restored. What is burdening you? Whatever it is, take it to the Lord in prayer. The Bible says that fasting draws us to closer to God. It allows us to give up something and focus on Him. You do not have to fast day and night.

Skip a meal and pray instead.

Listen to the burdens of your heart, He is willing to listen and give you what your heart desires if it is in His will. Pray and fast before the God of Heaven just as Nehemiah did.

Nehemiah was an amazing strategist. He gave different families responsibility for different sections of the wall. While they were building the wall, their adversaries tried every measure to defeat them. They bullied them, laughed at them, ridiculed them and threatened them. However, Nehemiah positioned guards to serve around the clock. The Israelites began to grow weary and discouraged, but, Nehemiah knew that God would fight their battles for them. They built with one hand and fought with the other. That is determination!

They rebuilt the wall that had been rubbish for a century and a half in a record 52 days. Please read, highlight, and record what took place at the dedication ceremony in Nehemiah 12:27-47. End today with a prayer regarding the burden and desire of your heart.

MEMORIZATION

Today we will begin memorizing the Epistles. There are 21 Epistles in the New Testament so get out your new index card and label it with Epistles and write out three columns of seven numerals per column, or make three cards; each with one column and seven numerals per card. Begin by writing the names of the first three epistles: Romans, I Corinthians and 2 Corinthians.

PRAYER OF AGREEMENT

Father, show the greatness of Your power on our behalf. My reader and I know there is no challenge too great for You to accomplish on our behalf. Thank You for moving all that must be moved or overcome for us, in Jesus' name, Amen.

Day 26

OPENING PRAYER

*L**ord, make me an example of Your attributes. I long for others to see You in me. Allow me to be to be the example that draws them to You, and changes their lives forever. Please make me the vessel for change in the lives of those around me, in Jesus' name I pray, Amen.*

LESSON: DANIEL

Daniel was a teenager when King Nebuchadnezzar took over Jerusalem and exiled the Israelites to Babylon. Daniel was a very smart young man. So much so in fact, that the head of the king's palace staff gave Daniel and three of his friends, Hananiah, Mishael and Azariah, positions in the king's court.

Daniel was brave and convicted to follow God. He knew that by being in the king's court he would have to eat the king's food and that would defile him. Therefore, he asked the steward if he and his friends could eat a diet of vegetables and water for 10 days and then they could be compared to the rest of the young men who were in the court. The steward liked Daniel and allowed them to be exempt. As we would expect, Daniel and his friends looked better than the rest of the boys at the end of the

10 days, so the steward permanently exempted them from the royal diet.

Already we see this young man puts God first. He was not willing to taint himself in God's eyes by partaking of the king's royal food. King Nebuchadnezzar was impressed with Daniel and his three friends. In comparison to the other boys, they were far superior in wisdom and knowledge.

King Nebuchadnezzar had a disturbing dream one night and decreed that unless the fortunetellers, magicians, dream interpreters or scorers could tell him his dream and interpret it they would all die. Daniel went to his friends and asked that they all pray and ask God to reveal the dream and its interpretation to them. That night Daniel received the interpretation from God. Immediately he blessed God.

Read and highlight Daniel 2:19-23. Daniel was able to tell the king what God had revealed to him. Read and highlight Daniel 2:46-49 and record the king's response in your Journal.

King Nebuchadnezzar had a statue built and required that everyone in Babylon worship the statue. Hananiah, Mishael and Azariah refused to worship at the altar. Certain fortunetellers went to the king and informed him the three were refusing to worship his golden statue. Upon learning this, the king was furious and had them thrown into a fiery furnace. When they looked into the furnace, after throwing the three young men in, they not only saw the three men walking around unharmed, there was a fourth man. The Scriptures are unclear who was in the furnace with Shadrach, Meshach, and Abednego, but many scholars say it was God himself and some even say it was Jesus.

Read and highlight Daniel 3:28-30. Record King Nebuchadnezzar's response when he learned the men were unharmed and showed no signs of even being in the furnace.

Nebuchadnezzar sent out a word to *"everyone, everywhere,"* what great deeds and miracles God has performed. However, he was still an evil man. He had a dream that he asked Daniel to interpret. After hearing the dream, Daniel knew it was about the king and did not want to tell him the interpretation. The king reassured him not to be scared of interpreting the dream. Daniel said, *"I wish this dream were about your enemies and its interpretation for your foes."* Read and highlight Daniel 4:20-37 and record in your Journal what takes place.

Nebuchadnezzar reconsidered after God humbled him. After his death Nebuchadnezzar's grandson, Belshazzar took over and threw a huge party during which he decided to drink out of the gold and silver goblets that Nebuchadnezzar had taken out of The Temple of God in Jerusalem.

God was furious at his actions and sent a hand (this may be where the handwriting is on the wall saying was coined)) to write on the wall. The hand wrote, *"Mene, Teqel, and Peres."* Daniel was an old man now and the king asked him to interpret the writing on the wall. He told the king that *"Mene"* meant that his days were numbered as king. *"Teqel"* meant that he was not measuring up to God's standards. *"Peres"* meant he would lose his kingdom and they would divide it and give it to the Medes and Persians. That very night the writing on the wall came true. Belshazzar died and Darius the Mede took over as king.

Daniel continued to have great favor. King Darius made him one of his vice-regents. Daniel stood above all the other vice-regents and governors and they were jealous. They went to the king and asked him to sign a decree stating that for 30 days no one could pray to any god except the king.

The king ordered anyone who disobeyed him thrown into the lion's den. When the king learned that Daniel disobeyed the decree he was very sorry and worked all day to reverse the decree. When he realized he could do nothing, Daniel was thrown into the lion's den. The king spent the night fasting. The next morning the king went to the lion's den and found Daniel still alive and unharmed. Daniel told the king that God had sent an angel to close the lion's mouth and so they were unable to harm him. The king ordered the people who had conspired against Daniel to be thrown into the lion's den and before they hit the floor, the lions devoured them.

Read and highlight Daniel 6:25-27 and record what the king decreed in your Journal.

Daniel was able to interpret dreams and he had several prophetic dreams.

Once again, we have witnessed an amazing common man who lived a life seeking and trusting God. The truth is, even his friends were God seekers. Think about that for a moment. It is not by chance that Daniel put that in his record of events. He did not just want you to know that these people went through the fire and God was with them and God saved them, he wanted you to know they were his friends. Why is this significant? Because your friends help define you.

Friends are important to your legacy. If you are friends with someone who is continually negative, what do you tend to become? If, however, you have friends that truly seek God when they are in the fire, what are you likely to do when you are in the fire? Please write a prayer of gratitude to God for sending you Christian friends. Write their names and meditate on the way they have influenced your walk.

MEMORIZATION

Add Galatians, Ephesians, and Philippians to your list of Epistles. Do not forget to review all your cards!

PRAYER OF AGREEMENT

Father, thank You for writing Your Word on the tablets of our hearts. My reader and I ask for wisdom and insight in every situation that confronts us. Allow us to feel Your guiding presence today, in Jesus' name, Amen.

Day 27

OPENING PRAYER

Heavenly Father, fulfill Your word in me today. As I study with You, allow those things You have predicted so long ago to permeate my heart and my being, and bring about the complete fulfillment of Your desires with me and through me, Amen.

LESSON: OLD TESTAMENT

Today we will complete our study of the Old Testament. The last book in the Old Testament is Malachi. This is God's final plea to the Israelites before the fulfillment of the prophecies given in the Old Testament. Our friends the Israelites were becoming very lazy in their worship.

An underlying current of disbelief was growing among them because God had not yet fulfilled His promise of sending them the descendant of David who would become their king. They believed God's Word, but they were anxious for Him to fulfill His promises.

Let us take a look at a few of the promises made in the Scriptures about the coming Messiah:

Isaiah 7:14 *"Watch for this: A girl who is presently a virgin will get pregnant. She'll bear a son, and name him Immanuel (God-With-Us)."*

Isaiah 11:1-5 *"A green Shoot will sprout from Jesse's stump, from his roots a budding Branch. The life-giving Spirit of God will hover over him, the Spirit that brings wisdom and understanding, The Spirit that gives direction and builds strength, the Spirit that instills knowledge and Fear-of-God. Fear-of-God will be all his joy and delight. He will not judge by appearances, won't decide on the basis of hearsay. He will judge the needy by what is right, render decisions on earth's poor with justice. His words will bring everyone to awed attention. A mere breath from his lips will topple the wicked. Each morning he'll pull on sturdy work clothes and boots, and build righteousness and faithfulness in the land."*

Read and highlight Isaiah 42:1-4.

Summarize these verses in your Journal.

Read and highlight Isaiah 53:1-12.

Summarize the event this passage records in your Journal.

Long before God sent the Messiah, He laid the foundation so His people would not miss His coming. He gave many exact accounts, hundreds and even thousands of years prior to His birth. We have seen His amazing provision repeatedly in the passages of the Old Testament. Now be prepared to see the prophecy come alive in the New Testament with the ultimate fulfillment and completion of the Blood Covenant established with Abraham.

Take time now to write a prayer thanking God for the fulfillment of His prophecies. How blessed we are to have eternal life because God sent His son, Jesus Christ, to die on the cross.

He did that with *you* in mind. He loves you that much. If you were the only one in the world, He would have still come!

Embrace His love. You have seen His love poured out on the Israelites. Now you can experience it for yourself. God sent His son so that you would be His forever.

MEMORIZATION

Today, add Colossians, 1 Thessalonians, and 2 Thessalonians to your Epistles card. Review as always and give yourself a pat on the back for your diligence!

PRAYER OF AGREEMENT

Lord, grant my reader and me prosperity today. Open the windows of heaven over us and release to us an abundant harvest, so great they we cannot contain it all. Thank You for meeting all of our needs, physically, emotionally, and spiritually, in Jesus' name, Amen.

Day 28

OPENING PRAYER

*F*ather, *as I study Your Word today, please reveal to me those things You want in my life. I ask You to grow the seed of Your own word in me, so that it will produce fruit that makes a difference in my life and in the lives of others, in the name of Jesus I pray, Amen.*

LESSON: OUR SAVIOR IS BORN

In biblical times, Hebrew marriage customs required parent-arranged marriages. Once the parents reached an agreement the couple was married. They would not live together until the full one-year waiting period was complete to ensure purity and faithfulness. If the bride became pregnant during that period, she was impure and they would arrange an annulment. The marriage of Joseph and Mary was an arrangement. Mary was in her one-year waiting period when the angel Gabriel came to her.

Read and highlight Luke 1:26-38 and summarize in your Journal what the angel said to Mary.

Note the words Gabriel used to greet Mary:

"Good morning!

You're beautiful with God's beauty,

Beautiful inside and out!

God be with you!"

This is God's greeting to you every day!

Mary was overcome with emotion. Her parents raised her to believe in God's Word and she knew the Messiah was coming, but now she was the one chosen by God, our God, to be the one who would give birth to Him. I am overwhelmed for her. However, Mary was confused, she had not been with a man; she was a virgin, so how could she get pregnant?

Gabriel told her the Holy Spirit was going to come upon her *"... Therefore the child you bring to birth will be called Holy, Son of God."* He also told her that Elizabeth was already pregnant even though she was old and had been barren.

What were Gabriel's final words (verses 36-38) before Mary accepted everything he said?

You see, *"Nothing is impossible with God."*

Before we move on, peek at Matthew's account of the birth of Jesus because it includes Joseph's response. Read and highlight Matthew 1:18-25. I would imagine Joseph was heartbroken to learn of Mary's pregnancy. Notice the Bible says he was *"determined to take care of things quietly so Mary would not be disgraced."* (What a good man).

The angel came to him and called him a "son of David" signifying and clarifying that Joseph was indeed a descendant of David. This is important because the Old Testament said the Messiah would be from David's lineage. Joseph believed the angel of the Lord and married Mary, but did not consummate the marriage until after Jesus' birth.

Let us turn back to Luke 1:39-45, where Mary went to stay with Elizabeth. Remember Elizabeth was carrying John, who would later prepare the way for Jesus. When Mary entered the home of Zachariah and Elizabeth and greeted them, the baby inside Elizabeth's tummy *"Leaped."* Even in the womb, John new to jump for joy at the coming Messiah.

Elizabeth had many beautiful words to say to Mary, but I love the last verse that says, *"Blessed woman, who believed what God said, believed every word would come true!"*

Mary believed.

Mary stayed with Elizabeth for three months and then returned home. She and Joseph went to Bethlehem in Judah, because Joseph was a descendant of David and Caesar Augustus ordered a census for his entire Empire. Since Joseph was a descendant of David and David was born in Bethlehem, he and Mary had to go and register in Bethlehem. While they were there, they gave birth to our Savior and Lord, Jesus Christ.

I am sure that you all remember the story of Jesus' birth. Have you ever thought about how prophetic it was that the angels appeared to sheepherders? Everything that God does is significant. He sent His angels to sheepherders who were protecting the sheep from harm, just as He sent our Shepherd to watch over us and save us from further harm. The shepherds also believed and it was confirmed when they saw Jesus swaddled in a blanket lying in a manger. They *"... let loose, glorifying and praising God for everything they had seen."*

Let us end our time today reflecting on several points. First, write down your current struggle in your Journal. After you write what you are struggling with, write these words:

"Nothing is impossible with God." Luke 1:37

Next, think about what you would do if you truly believed all the desires God has placed on your heart. Perhaps God has given you the desire to be married. Mary believed. That set her apart from many of us. The sheepherders believed. Abraham believed. Isaac believed. I could go on and on with characters from the Bible that acted on their faith. The only difference between then and now is that each one of us, as believers, have the gift of the Holy Spirit living inside of us prompting us.

We do not need a burning bush. We have the Spirit of the living God dwelling inside of us waiting for us to believe the promptings. As we end today, I ask that you record all the desires of your heart. Spend time earnestly searching for those desires. Pray and ask God to help you believe the promptings. He wants to move in you in magnificent ways, just let Him.

MEMORIZATION

Review all your books up to this point, and add 1 Timothy, 2 Timothy and Titus to your Epistles. If you have fallen behind do not be upset with yourself or give up, there is plenty of time to catch up.

PRAYER OF AGREEMENT

Lord, if my reader has yet to experience the new birth, I ask You to bring them to a place of repentance and crowning You Lord. Make all things new for them. Thank You that in Christ, old things are gone and everything is made new. Whatever new thing my reader needs, whatever new life he or she wants, I thank You for providing it, in Jesus' name, Amen.

Day 29

OPENING PRAYER

L ord God, thank You for being there when I have not spent the time with You the way that I should. Thank You for patiently waiting for me to come to the end of myself, and waiting for me to realize I cannot go on without You. I set myself to be completely united to You each and every day. Amen.

LESSON: JOHN THE BAPTIST PREPARES THE WAY

The account of John the Baptist in the Book of Luke was such a revelation and confirmation of God's divine plan. His parents, Zachariah and Elizabeth, were from the priestly descendants of Aaron. In lesson 22, we learned that King David established all the plans for worship. Then 1 Chronicles 23:32 confirmed Aaron as the leader of *"everything that has to do with worship."* If you look at 1 Chronicles 24:10, you will see that Abijah was the eighth family selected. Read and highlight Luke 1:5 and you will see that Zachariah was from that family division. Zachariah was from a long family legacy of God-Seekers and vital part of God's plan for worshipping Him.

Read and highlight Luke 1:5-25.

We learn that Zachariah and Elizabeth *"Together lived honorably before God, careful in keeping with the ways of the commandments and enjoying a clear conscience before God."* I stressed "together" because they made a choice to live an honorable life in spite of the fact that they both desperately wanted children. They must have had endless conversations about God's will, but they stood in agreement to continue to seek and serve Him in spite of their disappointment. They did not let bitterness set in.

Zachariah was performing his priestly duties in the sanctuary, which would be the only time in his life that he would perform this task, when an angel of God named Gabriel appeared.

Record what the angel tells Zachariah from Luke 1:13-15 in your Journal.

Because of Zachariah and Elizabeth's faithfulness, the angel of the Lord told Zachariah that they were going to have a son and his name would be John. The angel also predicted six aspects of John's character - he will be a joy and delight, he will achieve great stature with God, he will never drink wine or other fermented drinks, he will be filled with the Holy Spirit from birth, he will bring many Israelites back to God and he will prepare the way for Jesus (*"He'll get the people ready for God"*). Read and highlight Malachi 3:1. John the Baptist fulfilled this prophecy.

Unfortunately, Zachariah was in complete disbelief. He said there was no way they were going to have a baby. *"I am old and by the way she is no spring chicken!"* Do you remember a similar conversation with our Old Testament friends Abraham and Sarah? Because of Zachariah's disbelief, he was unable to speak until John was born. Look at verse 20. Whose time were they on?

Do you have a deep yearning for something God has not yet allowed to happen? Psalms 37:4 says, *"Delight yourself in the Lord, and He will give you the desires of your heart."* Learn from our forefathers to continue to seek and serve the Lord in spite of the feeling of rejection. Do not allow the enemy to keep you in a negative, disbelieving state. He is the father of this world and the father of lies. Do not listen to those lies. Instead, focus on God's truth. He is able to provide exceedingly and abundantly in His time!

John was born and there was much joy. Zachariah, rendered silent by the Lord, was able to speak, just as Gabriel predicted, after John was born. People were amazed and said, *"What will become of this child? Clearly, God has his hand in this."*

Read and highlight Luke 1:67-79 and record anything you believe is significant in your Journal.

John lived in the desert until he received a message from God directing him to begin his public ministry. John preached about a *"baptism of life change"* that would lead to the *"forgiveness of sins."* John's ministry amazed the people. In fact, some were beginning to believe he was the Messiah. Read and highlight Luke 3:16-17 for John's response. John knew what his role was. Verse 18 says, *"the message continued and gave people strength and heart."*

John even baptized Jesus, witnessed the Holy Spirit settling on Jesus, and heard the voice of the Father identify Jesus as His Son. Not long after this, King Herod, who felt threatened by

John's message, put John in prison where he continued to minister until he was beheaded.

In our quest to leave a legacy of faith, we must not overlook the fact that our actions today have a direct impact on the future. If you are struggling with an area of disbelief or repeated sin, I beg you to get it right before God. You want to have a clear conscience before God so that He can reveal what He wants you to do. God put us on this earth to serve Him. He has a plan and a purpose. Walk boldly and blamelessly before Him. Be still and quiet before Him often so you do not miss His instruction. You may give birth to the next John the Baptist. You may be the next John the Baptist!

Submit yourself to God to accomplish the things He wants to accomplish in you today. Remember Zachariah only performed his priestly duty once in his life, which was the day God revealed to him that he would have a son who would prepare the way for Jesus. You never know what He has in store for you. Listen and walk expectantly.

MEMORIZATION

Include Philemon, Hebrews, and James today, and review your other books as usual.

PRAYER OF AGREEMENT

Lord, I pray Psalms 37:4 for my reader today. May we both delight in You, as You give us the desires of our hearts. Thank You for fulfilling the most intense yearnings of our hearts, and providing for all our needs, Amen.

Day 30

OPENING PRAYER

*F*ather, *I ask for patience and the ability to persevere as I begin this study today. I thank You for always giving me strength when I am weak, and carrying me when I am too tired to go on by myself. Help me to be a strength to others as I continue on my walk with You, Amen.*

LESSON: THE BEGINNING OF JESUS' MINISTRY

What an amazing journey we have been on so far. I commend you on making it to day 30 and for being so diligent in your studies and I hope it has become abundantly clear that God is waiting on us to seek Him and to be obedient to His call. I hope you took time to study the Scriptures provided for you in yesterday's study that pointed to the coming King. We are going to begin our study with the fulfillment of some of those prophecies.

The New Testament Book of Matthew, written by Matthew (also known as "Levi") and is one of the Gospels, which means "Good News." He wrote this Gospel to help Jews see that Jesus was the Messiah. The Jews were very familiar with the Old Testament prophecies. Matthew quoted the Old Testament 45 times. They spent much time reading, memorizing, and studying the Scriptures; therefore, the Jewish people knew the coming Messiah would be an heir of King David. Matthew began his writing with a genealogy demonstrating Jesus' relation to King David beginning with Abraham. Review and highlight Matthew 1:1-17.

Jesus is far different from the king that the Jews were expecting. They were familiar with the role of kings. They were looking for a strong ruler. They were expecting a king that would defeat the Romans, take the worldly throne, and set the Jews above all other peoples. They were looking for all the things that Jesus was not.

Just as God selected the most unlikely people to carry out His desires in the Old Testament, Jesus also selected common people to apprentice during His time on earth, so they could continue His teachings after He was gone. The first four people God chose were fisherman. He said the same thing to each of them: *"Come with me and I will make you a fisher of men and women."* All four, Simon, (Peter) Andrew, James and John, were quick to leave their work and follow Christ.

Matthew was also one of Jesus' disciples. Matthew walked with Jesus, witnessed many miracles, and listened intently to his teachings. The first event Matthew mentions after the birth of Jesus is His baptism. John the Baptist was in the Jordan River when Jesus appeared. He had been baptizing and teaching people about God's Kingdom. He explained to the Sadducees and Pharisees that they could not get into God's Kingdom just because they were Abraham's children. Birthright, he explained, had no bearing; it was about faith in God. Read and highlight

Matthew 3:13-17 and record what happened when Jesus came out of the water.

Jesus' baptism marked the beginning of his ministry. The next account mentioned in Matthew is about the devil testing Jesus. Read and highlight Matthew 4:1-11. What did Jesus do to prepare for his test? When the devil tested Jesus, what did He do each time?

After John baptized Jesus and His ministry begins, He is tested. This symbolizes our ministry in Christ. Becoming a Christian does not automatically give you an exemption from the devil. In fact, the devil is going to tempt you even more. The difference between Jesus' temptation and our temptation is that Jesus was tempted, but without sin. Notice that Jesus combated the devil with God's Word. Write down word for word the temptations and then the Scriptures that Jesus used.

Jesus prepared for His test by fasting. Jesus knew the devil was going to tempt Him and He prepared by denying Himself. Jesus was able to counter everything the devil tempted Him with by proclaiming God's Truth. This is a wonderful prescription for our personal temptations. Get ready; you will be tempted when you begin your ministry. God said to lean on Him and arm yourself with His Truth and He will carry you. Jesus began His teachings in the Book of Matthew with the Sermon on the Mount. This sermon is in Chapters 5, 6 and 7.

Beatitudes (Matthew 5:1-12): This word derived from the Latin word "Beatus" which means blessed or happy. Please write all nine, found in Matthew 5:3-12.

Salt and Light (Matthew 5:13-16): Why did God place us here?

God's Law Completed (Matthew 5:17-48): Jesus says, *"I'm not here to demolish the law but to complete it. I am going to put it all together, pull it all together in a vast panorama. God's law is more real and lasting than the stars in the sky and the ground at your feet."* Matthew 5:17-18.

Murder

Adultery and Divorce

Empty Promises

Love Your Enemies

Prayer (Matthew 6:1-18):

The World Is Not a Stage

Pray with Simplicity – The Lord's Prayer

A Life of God-Worship (Matthew 6:19-34):

A Simple Guide for Behavior (Matthew 7:1-12):

Being and Doing (Matthew 7:13-29):

Jesus continued His journey by healing the sick, raising the dead, enabling the blind to see and making the deaf hear. The teaching I would like you to record is the charge Jesus gave the 12 disciples before he sent them out. Please read and highlight Matthew 10:5-42. Read, highlight and write this in your Journal as if Jesus is speaking directly to you - because He is! Meditate on these words and thank God for His instruction.

MEMORIZATION

We are in the final stretch! Add 1 Peter and 2 Peter to your Epistles and see if you can recite all your Old Testament Books twice today. You are doing super, keep it up!

PRAYER OF AGREEMENT

Lord, just as Jesus prepared for His mission on this earth, prepare my reader and me for the calling You have on our lives. May our earthly missions be completely fulfilled, in Jesus' name, Amen.

Day 31

OPENING PRAYER

My Father in Heaven, I ask You to help me to continue to be a shining light. I ask You to give me the courage to reach into the places where people are hurting and bring them Your delivering light. Help me to always give You the glory, and to have the strength to stand against all the attacks of the enemy, in the name of Jesus I pray, Amen

LESSON: THE LIFE AND TEACHINGS OF OUR SAVIOR

Before Jesus sent the 12 disciples out, He instructed them and He charged them: *"This is large work that I've called you into, but don't be overwhelmed by it. It is best to start small. Give a cool cup of water to someone who is thirsty, for instance. The smallest act of giving or receiving makes you a true apprentice."* Matthew 10:41-42.

As we seek to know God, we continue to learn how to follow Christ's example. In Mark 8:34-37 Jesus tells the crowd that anyone intending to follow Him has to let Him lead. I like to use the analogy of Jesus being in the driver's seat of our lives.

I was in the driver's seat for most of my life. Jesus was a passenger in the front seat sometimes, but most of the time He was in the back seat or trying to get my attention from outside the vehicle. I thought I was in control of my own life. It was only when my life started spinning out of control, and I realized I could do nothing on my own that I asked Jesus to take control of the wheel.

Now I enjoy being a passenger. I love looking out the window not knowing our next destination, but trusting Him to get me there. The only road map that I need is one that says, "Trust and obey." I am learning to do just that. I hope you are too. It is not an easy ride. In fact, Jesus goes on to say that, we must embrace suffering. God is at the wheel and He promises He will never leave us. Thank you Lord!

There is a concept the Message version translates as: "The Great Reversal" and we find it in Mark 10:31. It says, *"Many who are first will end up last, and the last first."* In this world, the people that are first are wealthy and appear to have it all. Jesus is saying that those people will find it very hard to get into the kingdom of God because they value their worldly treasures much more than being a servant of God. Read and highlight Mark 10:43-45. Record what you have to do to be great. What did Jesus come to do?

Read and highlight Mark 12:29-31 and record the most important commandment in your Journal.

Read and highlight Luke 6:17-38. When does God bless us? How should we live our lives?

LESSON EXERCISES

What further instructions did Jesus give us in Luke 9:62?

According to Luke 1-13, how should we pray?

Today we learned to start small and let Jesus be the driver. We need to be last on Earth in order to be first in Heaven. End our session today thanking God for His Son and the simple instructions that He left for us. Finally, do something small for God's kingdom today!

MEMORIZATION

Add 1 John, 2 John, and 3 John today. Review all your cards. It is getting easier right.

PRAYER OF AGREEMENT

Lord, guide my reader and me moment by moment as we seek to do Your will. May we be transformed into Your image. In Jesus' name, Amen.

Day 32

OPENING PRAYER

Father, help me to see the opportunities to share You and Your Word with others today. I submit myself; use me to bless others and spread Your Word and Your wisdom, Your healing power and Your ability to deliver hurting people, in the name of Jesus, Amen

LESSON: THE LIFE AND TEACHINGS OF OUR SAVIOR

Hostility toward Jesus was mounting. He had only been teaching a short period and yet His teachings and healings were making the Jewish leaders very angry. They were watching and listening to His every move. They did not believe He was the Messiah and yet they did not understand how He was able to do the things He could do. One of the central issues the Jewish leaders were using against Jesus was that He was healing people on the Sabbath.

Read and highlight John 5:15-18.

Jesus informed them that His "Father" was working on the Sabbath and He was going to as well. Up until this time, they were out to expose Jesus. When he claimed that his Father was God, they seethed with anger because Jesus was making Himself equal with God. The Jewish leaders now believed they had ample cause to kill Jesus. He told them that He, "the Son", was not self-initiated nor was He independent of the Father. His Father, doing exactly what the Father willed Him to do, in fact directed him.

Jesus said "... *My purpose is not to get your vote, and not to appeal to mere human testimony. I'm speaking to you this way so that you will be saved."* John 5:34. You can almost feel Jesus' frustration with these people who claimed to be religious. They made a point to let Him, and everyone else know that they knew the Scriptures and spent a lifetime studying God's Word.

Yet, as Jesus pointed out - they missed the central point of the entire Old Testament.

Jesus said, *"If you believed, really believed, what Moses said, you would believe Me. He wrote of Me. If you won't take seriously what he wrote, how can I expect you to take seriously what I speak?"* John 5:46-47.

Jesus taught in a manner not used before. He used parables to illustrate His teachings. These parables often left people, even his disciples, confused. Jesus explained in one parable that He was the bread of life. He told a crowd that they should not waste their time on perishable food, but instead should focus on the food that nourished their life forever. This food can only come from the "Son of Man", He said.

The people were confused and told Jesus, they would believe in Him if they could see what He was capable of doing. They went further to say that, Moses gave their ancestors manna from heaven for 40 years. The truth, Jesus explained, was that God the Father supplied the Israelites with manna, not Moses. In fact, Jesus goes on to explain that God is offering each of them bread from heaven.

Jesus said, *"I am the Bread of Life. The person who aligns with Me hungers no more and thirsts no more, ever. I have told you this explicitly because even though you have seen Me in action, you don't really believe Me. Every person the Father gives Me eventually comes running to Me. And once that person is with Me, I hold on and don't let go. I came down from heaven, not to follow My own whim, but to accomplish the will of the One Who sent Me. This, in a nutshell, is that will: that everything handed over to Me by the Father be completed - not a single detail missed- and at the wrap-up time I have everything and everyone put together, upright and whole. This is what My Father wants: that anyone who sees the Son and trusts Who He is and what He does and then aligns with Him will enter real life, eternal life. My part is to put them on their feet alive and whole at the completion of time"* John 6:35-40.

Do you hear the urgency in Jesus' words? The Jewish leaders did not believe who Jesus claimed to be and they argued about everything He taught. It is interesting that the same lack of belief and fighting about Jesus still exists today. All we have to do is believe - not bits and pieces, but the entire love story.

As we end today, reread John 6:35-40. Focus on the fact that you are a gift from the maker of Heaven and Earth (John 6:65). Meditate on these words: *"Every person the Father gives me eventually comes running to me. And once that person is with me, I hold on and don't let go."*

Picture Jesus holding His arms out for you and you running as fast as you can into His precious arms. Once you get to Him, He grabs you, holds you, and tells you that He will never let you go.

MEMORIZATION

Review all your cards, and add Jude to your list of Epistles. We are almost to the end!

PRAYER OF AGREEMENT

Father, fulfill 2 Corinthians 9:12 in my reader's and my lives that we may not come behind in any gift. Enrich our lives, talents and our skills to accomplish all that You have called us to do, in Jesus' name, Amen.

Day 33

OPENING PRAYER

L ord, I desire a more intimate relationship with You. I long to know You more and more and to see Your face. I ask You to reveal more of Yourself as I seek You, and as I study Your Word and spend quiet time with You. In the name of Jesus I pray, Amen.

LESSON: THE FINAL TEACHINGS OF OUR SAVIOR

Today, we get to take a glimpse of Jesus' teachings, just hours prior to His arrest and conviction. Let us enter the upper room where the disciples gathered with Jesus for the Passover Feast.

They must have been thinking about the amazing journey they had the privilege to go on with Jesus. They were his chosen disciples; hand selected to tell the world for generations to come about the love of Jesus. They saw His perfection first hand. They felt the very presence of God in flesh. They saw Jesus repeatedly do things they would not have expected.

Now in the upper room, Jesus began to wash their feet. This act made Simon Peter very uncomfortable. In fact, He told Jesus that He would never wash his feet. So, Jesus in His sweet way said in John 13:8 *"If I don't wash you, you can't be a part of what I'm doing."* In John 13:9 Peter says *"Not only my feet, then. Wash my hands! Wash my head!"*

I often refer to myself as the modern day Peter. There have been so many times that I have spoken or acted before I thought. Peter was guilty of that on many occasions. However, Jesus loved him in spite of his shortcomings. Jesus loves us all in spite of our shortcomings. Jesus went on to tell Peter He was not concerned about hygiene, but holiness. He also told Peter that he would understand the meaning of this later. Peter missed the spiritual lesson that Jesus was teaching, but he had a deep desire to connect with Jesus.

Think about that for a moment. How many times do we miss the deep spiritual meaning of something? However, if we have the desire to walk with Jesus, He overlooks those shortcomings and tells us we will understand the meaning later. Nevertheless, we must continue to seek Him.

Read and highlight John 13:12-17. Summarize this passage in your Journal and relate the teaching to your life.

The act of washing the disciple's feet was significant to Jesus' departure. He needed the disciples to understand that they were merely servants of the Master. Jesus gave the disciples this visual demonstration to serve as an example of the humble service Christians were, and are, to provide for one another. Jesus told the disciples in John 13:17

"If you understand what I am telling you act like it — and live a blessed life." Jesus was trying to explain to the disciples that true joy comes through obedient service.

Let us end today by journaling about the feet you have washed on behalf of our Master and Lord. Write the humble services you provided for fellow believers and nonbelievers. Write also about the way other believers have washed your feet. Record a prayer for the people God is going to put in your path and ask Him right now to give you strength and wisdom to be a humble servant. Thank Him for inviting you into His inner circle and His upper room as He did the disciples. Be obedient in your service to Him so you can experience true joy.

MEMORIZATION

Today is your final day for writing down the Books of the Bible. Take out one final index card, and write Prophetic Revelation at the top of the card and then write Revelation as the one and only book on this card. Congratulations, you have finished the writing part of the memorization exercises. Do not forget to review all the books and see if you can recite them all the way through!

PRAYER OF AGREEMENT

Father, grant my reader and I servants' hearts that we will delight in serving others. In Jesus' name I pray, Amen.

Day 34

OPENING PRAYER

Father, may nothing separate me from You today. I purposely move closer to You, and I know You have promised that when I do You will move closer to me. I thank You for Your close presence, in the name of Jesus, Amen.

LESSON: THE FINAL TEACHINGS OF OUR SAVIOR

Let us continue in John 13 today. Jesus and the disciples are still in the upper room and Jesus just finished washing their feet. They were still somewhat confused about what He was trying to teach them and were trying to figure it all out when Jesus proceeded to tell them that not everyone present at the table would receive God's blessing. He further went on to reassure them He knew exactly who would attempt to deceive Him. He told them it had to happen this way in order to fulfill Scripture.

Jesus was referring to Psalm 41:9, *"The one who ate bread at My table turned his heel against Me."* Later the disciples would remember this and realize that He fulfilled the Scripture, which would add to their faith in Jesus. Peter motioned to John, who was sitting next to Jesus and asked him to inquire who among them would betray him. Read, highlight, and summarize what took place in John 13:26-30 in your Journal.

Imagine the tension in the air in the room at that moment. The other disciples had no idea what Judas had done or what he was about to do. After Judas took the bread, the Bible says Satan entered him.

Have you ever allowed the enemy to enter you metaphorically speaking?

I am not proud to say it, but I have. I still struggle with allowing the enemy to control my emotions and my tongue and use me as a weapon against others. It is important that we make sure to turn our eyes upon Jesus and submit completely to God when the enemy attempts to control us. James 4:7 says to submit to God and resist the devil. I like to say that I want to be a vessel of God and not as a weapon of the enemy.

What happened fulfilled Scripture, even though his actions troubled Jesus. He loved Judas. He had hand selected Judas. He grieved over the spiritual hardness that sin had produced in Judas. There are many things in our lives that the enemy uses to make us spiritually hard. Our job is to seek God and know that when we seek Him, He is there waiting for us.

He longs for you to go rushing to Him and tell Him how sorry you are for allowing the enemy to use you. He grieves when you make wrong choices, but He rejoices when you make the right choice; and the right choice is to run to His waiting arms today, this minute. Whatever your circumstance, run boldly to Him, tell Him how sorry you are, He will forgive you, and He will rejoice over you.

After Judas left, Jesus continued His teaching. Read and highlight John 13:33-38. How did Jesus address the 11 disciples in verse 33?

Jesus is not using the word "children" here to be demeaning. It is actually an endearing term, which further demonstrated His love for them. Not only was He demonstrating His love for the disciples by calling them "children", perhaps He was also making this statement so they would remember the words He spoke to them earlier on their journey. Look at Luke 18:15-17. Please write what Luke 18:17 says in your Journal.

The NIV Study Bible elaborates on this verse by explaining that childlike faith means following Jesus: "*With total dependence, full trust, frank openness and complete sincerity.*" How simple is that? Think about each one of those for a moment: total dependence, full trust, frank openness and complete sincerity. I began journaling my prayers around those statements.

Every time I read something like this, I feel privileged to learn a major secret. The only difference is I get to share this secret!

What was the new command that Jesus gave the disciples in John 13:34-35?

Love is the distinguishing characteristic that sets the disciples and each one of us apart. Not just any love. The love that Jesus was talking about is the love that He demonstrated and the love that God the Father demonstrated by sending Jesus to die so that we may have everlasting life.

It is unconditional.

We will never be able have or give the same kind of love that Jesus did, but we can strive to provide this type of love in our lives.

In order to better understand the type of love that Christ gives and the type of love that He wants us to strive for, we need to read 1 Corinthians 13. This is a scripture that we have all heard a thousand times at weddings and other events, but now I want you to apply them to our lesson. These words describe Our Lord and Savior Jesus Christ. Jesus is God in flesh. He made us in His image. When people describe others as Christ like, this is what they mean. Write them down. Etch them on your heart. Memorize them. Meditate on them. Apply them in your daily life.

With total dependence, full trust, frank openness and complete sincerity pray and ask God to help you display this kind of love so people will recognize you are a disciple of Christ.

In Christ, let us: *"Trust steadily in God, hope unswervingly, love extravagantly."*

LESSON EXERCISES

Complete the following statements on love from 1 Corinthians 13:3-7:

1. Love never
2. Love cares more for others than
3. Love does not want what it
4. Love does not
5. Doesn't have a
6. Doesn't force itself

7. Isn't always

8. Doesn't fly off

9. Doesn't keep score of

10. Doesn't revel when others

11. Takes pleasure in the flowering

12. Puts up with

13. Trusts in God

14. Always looks for

15. Never looks

16. But keeps going

MEMORIZATION

You did it! Yesterday you completed your cards and got through all the names of all the Books of the Bible. Now, as you recite and review them all, try some new approaches. Hand the cards to a friend and ask them to test your knowledge. Have them ask you which book comes after this one, or which book comes before that one. I am so proud of you!

PRAYER OF AGREEMENT

Father, help my reader and I to walk in love all the days of our lives. May we always rejoice when truth prevails, and believe the best of every person, quick to forgive. I ask this in Jesus' name, Amen.

Day 35

OPENING PRAYER

God in Heaven, please help me today to keep my mind and thoughts on You and not on the circumstances. I trust in You to keep me in perfect peace, according to Your Word, and to lift me above all worldly worries, in the name of Jesus, Amen.

LESSON: THE FINAL HOURS OF CHRIST

Today, begin by reading and highlighting John 14:15-31.

The very first passage here is vital to our relationship with Christ. If we love Christ, we will obey His commands. Reflect back on our last lesson where we learned about His new command. Do you remember what it was? Write it down in your Journal.

We are to love one another just as Christ loved us. However, our love for Christ cannot be set apart from obedience. Obedience is the critical element to live fully in God's will. Jesus went on to say that in order to help us remain obedient, God the Father will provide us with *"... another Friend so that you will always have someone with you."*

I remember the first time I read this passage from The Message translation. I was on my back patio praying and asking, (begging, really) God to help me understand friendship. When I opened my Bible and turned to this section, it brought me to my knees. Tears came to my eyes and I thanked Him profusely for His Word. I had read the passage in other translations many times, but none of the translations referred to the Holy Spirit as "Friend."

I sought God for guidance on friendship and just as we have learned in this study, when you seek Him you will find Him. This passage taught me that my true Friend is the Helper and Counselor God placed inside of me when I became a follower of His. He is the Friend who will never leave me.

Jesus went on to describe this Friend as *the Spirit of Truth.*" The world cannot accept the Spirit of Truth because it does not see the Spirit nor does it know the Spirit of God.

Write the last five words in verse 17: _____
_____ _____ _____ _____!
Notice the word *"in."* The reason we emphasize this word is that in the Old Testament the Spirit would come to certain believers to enable them to carry out special assignments by God and then leave again.

The Spirit of Truth Jesus was referring to resides in each believer forever. The Spirit does not come just for special occasions. The Spirit comes and stays permanently, and this sets us apart from the rest of the world. Through this indwelling Friend, we can display the light of Christ to a dark and hopeless world.

The Spirit of Truth (commonly referred to as the Holy Spirit) plays an essential role in seeking and knowing God. The Holy Spirit completes the "Trinity."

The term Trinity is not a Scriptural term, but rather is the name of the Doctrine most Christians use when referring to God the Father, God the Son and God the Holy Spirit, altogether. "Tri"- means three and "Unity" means one; Tri + Unity = Trinity. The Doctrine of the Trinity is a way of recognizing that God is three Persons who are one in perfect unity and agreement of purpose and doctrine.

God the Son (Jesus) is fully, completely God. God the Father is fully, completely God. In addition, God the Holy Spirit is fully, completely God. Yet there is only one God. To be complete in God, we must believe and receive His Son (John 3:16). Once we accept Jesus as our Lord and Savior, then we receive the Holy Spirit or the "Friend."

It is truly amazing that God resides inside of us. The same God that spoke to Abraham, Isaac, Jacob and Moses does not speak to us from up above, but lives inside us.

Read and highlight 1 Corinthians 3:16.

According to 1 Corinthians 2:15 the Holy Spirit gives us the ability to know everything that "... *God's Spirit is doing.*"

John 16:12-15 says that when the "Friend" comes "... *He will take you by the hand and guide you into all the truth there is.*"

The primary role of the Holy Spirit is to bear "witness" of Jesus Christ. (John 15:26, 16:14) He ministers the truth of Jesus Christ to our hearts. The Holy Spirit acts as a Christian's teacher and reveals God's will to all believers.

God gave the Holy Spirit to us in order to produce his character in our life. The Holy Spirit brings gifts into our lives which include love, joy, peace, patience, kindness, goodness, faithfulness, gentleness and self-control in a way we cannot do on our own (Gal. 5:22-23NIV).

Rather than demanding that we try to love and be patient and kind on our own, God asks us to rely on Him to produce these qualities in our lives. As Christians, we are to take hold of this gift and live it out in every aspect of our lives. We are all unique and so we should not compare ourselves with others, but live out the life that the Spirit directs us individually to live (Galatians 5:25-26).

God has provided everything we need through the Spirit that is in each of us. Please conclude today by reading and highlighting Romans chapter 12. Spend time meditating on this passage and on the Friend God has given you.

MEMORIZATION

Are you having trouble memorizing the names of the Books of the Bible? Remember your inner Friend! Ask God to help!

PRAYER OF AGREEMENT

Lord, according to Matthew 18:18-19 fill my reader and myself with all the fruits of righteousness, and with the knowledge that according to Philippians 4:9 You are meeting all their needs according to Your riches in Glory in Christ Jesus, Amen.

Day 36

OPENING PRAYER

Dear Lord, as I get ready to spend time in Your Word and do my Bible Study today, I submit to You and Your Will for my life. I submit to You as the master craftsman of my life, and I trust in You to fashion me into a tool You can use to the fullest, in the name of Jesus, Amen.

LESSON: THE FINAL HOURS OF CHRIST

Read and highlight John 15.

This is one of my absolute favorite passages in the Bible. I have spent a lot of time reading, highlighting and studying this passage. Let us take a walk with Jesus and the disciples through the vineyard and listen as Jesus explains the relationship between God, The Son of Man and us, His beloved people.

Record with me John 15: 1-4: *"I am the _____ _____ and my Father is the _____. He cuts off every branch that doesn't _____ _____. And every branch that is grape-bearing He prunes back _____ _____ _____ _____ _____ _____."* The next verse says that we are already pruned back *"... _____ _____ _____ _____ _____ _____."* Jesus goes on to say, *"Live in Me. Make your home* *in Me just as I do in you. In the same way that a branch can't bear grapes by itself, but only by being joined to the vine,* _____ _____ _____

_____ _____ _____ _____ _____ _____

_____."

What a beautiful illustration. Can you picture the vineyard? I envision it in a beautiful, lavish setting where the grape vines are bountiful and full of grapes. The farmer tends to his vineyard with much love. He expects a plentiful harvest. He anticipates every branch to bear much fruit. He is not satisfied with only a few fruit. The farmer takes every branch in his hand and prunes any branch that is bearing grapes so that it will produce more grapes.

Do you see the connection? Our Heavenly Father loves us so much that He is not satisfied with a little fruit. He desires for us to have an abundant harvest. He wants us to display that harvest, so the world can see. Turn to Galatians 5:22-23 and record with me how God displays fruit in our lives. *"But what happens when we live God's way? He brings _____ to our lives, much the same way that _____ appears in an _____----things like_____for others, _____ about life, _____. We develop a willingness to stick with things, a sense of _____ in the heart, and a conviction that a basic _____ permeates things and people. We find ourselves involved in _____ _____, not needing to _____ our way in life, able to marshal and direct _____ _____."*

These verses demonstrate the Fruit of the Spirit. This is the fruit that God desires for us to produce. The NIV says it this way:

"The Fruit of the Spirit is love, joy, peace, patience, kindness, goodness, faithfulness, gentleness and self-control."

Before we go on, I want you to meditate on this concept for a moment. You are the branch, Jesus is the vine and God is the farmer. Think about a situation in your life where you know God is pruning you. Thank Him for this because it will eventually lead to an abundant harvest of spiritual fruit that will benefit His kingdom.

After Jesus talks about the relationship of the Vine and the Branches, he proceeds to talk about love and obedience. (John 15:9-15) Jesus tells the disciples that He has loved them the way God loved Jesus. He goes on to tell them: *"Make yourselves at home in my love. If you keep my commands, you'll remain intimately at home in my love. This is the very best way to love. Put your life on the line for your _____. You are my _____ when you do the things I command you. I'm no longer calling you servants, because servants don't understand what their master is thinking and planning. No, I've named you _____ because I've let you in on everything I've heard from my Father."*

This passage builds on what Jesus taught about bearing much fruit. You cannot bear fruit if you do not love. Love is the root of everything. Take a quick look at what you wrote about pruning. Does the problem stem from a lack of true love? If so, you are going to have a difficult time producing an abundant harvest. Your Heavenly Father knows your heart. He knows your struggle and desires to assist you in overcoming the situation. Only He can help you. Turn to Him. Lay all your burdens at His feet and ask Him to replace those burdens with the Fruit of the Spirit.

Let us end today with a note about John 15:16. Has there ever been a time in your life when you really wanted to be in a group but you did not make the cut? When I was in college, I wanted to be involved with a group called Fashion Board. I went through "rush" very confidently only to learn that they did not select me. I was devastated.

How blessed we are that Jesus chose us. Thank you Jesus!

All I need to know and remember is that my God chose *me*. He chose all of me. He did the same for you. He chose us just the way we are. Since He chose us, He expects us to get busy and bear fruit. The plump, ripe, great tasting, great smelling, beautiful kind. Once you bear fruit, God's word goes on to say, "*... whatever you ask the Father in relation to Me, He gives you.*"

How can you bear the fruit that God asks you to bear? Do you remember what God told Abraham in lesson 5? "On your feet get moving!" This is our charge now. Get busy and bear fruit that will be stored up in Heaven. Do not be afraid to ask, "*whatever you want in relation to Jesus*" because God's Word says He will give it to you.

MEMORIZATION

Review and recite your Books of the Bible all the way through. If you have already mastered the entire list and can say them easily, maybe you can challenge yourself a little and see if you can say them backwards!

PRAYER OF AGREEMENT

Heavenly Father, my reader and I come before You today with humble hearts to ask You to forgive us for anything we have done that would prevent us from a fruitful harvest. We long to experience and reproduce the love, joy, peace, patience, kindness, goodness, faithfulness, gentleness and self-control that comes from our abiding in You. Help us love unconditionally, forgive those who wrong us and love them the way You do. We pray this in the name of Your precious Son, Jesus, Amen.

Day 37

OPENING PRAYER

Heavenly Father, please help me today to walk by Your Word and not my own feelings. I set myself in faith to do as You would have me do, say what You would have me say, and think what You would have me think. In the name of Jesus I pray, Amen.

LESSON: CHRIST'S FINAL PRAYER

Jesus knew what was about to take place.

He knew He was about to fulfill a major prophecy given by Isaiah 700 years earlier. Read and highlight Isaiah chapter 53. My son David had to memorize this Scripture for his Bible Class when he was in fourth grade. He would recite it every day. It never occurred to me what this passage meant, but after I heard it repeatedly, it began to make sense and gave me goose bumps.

Isaiah was prophesying the life events and purpose of Jesus Christ our Savior. I had the opportunity to sit with David and explain what the passage meant and I think that made it real. Instead of just memorizing a chapter of the Bible, he could now recite the events that would forever change *our* lives.

Read and highlight John chapter 17. What an example Jesus set for us. Before the Romans seized Jesus, He petitioned the Father, (our Father) for Himself first, then the Apostles and finally future believers. Take the time to soak in every word Jesus spoke. Place yourself at His feet and listen to His sweet words as He prays. Meditate on these words. Record what God says to you through His words in Isaiah chapter 53 and John chapter 17.

MEMORIZATION

Without looking first, can you name all the Epistles in order? Try right now. Now see if you can tell me the five Books of the Law. Can you now recite the Prophets? What about the Historical Books? What is the last Book of the Bible? Can you name the Gospels? Keep up the great work!

PRAYER OF AGREEMENT

Lord, teach us to pray as Jesus prayed. My reader and I ask You to instruct and guide us in the ways You want us to approach You so that our times with You, and the prayers we pray, will be not only intimate, but effective. In the name of Jesus, we pray, Amen.

Day 38

OPENING PRAYER

*L*ord, I am asking you to move in my heart today as I give myself completely to You, and I thank You in advance for guiding all my steps and keeping me in Your will. I submit to Your Holy Spirit and Your teaching all day long in all circumstances and in every situation. In the name of Jesus I pray, Amen.

LESSON: COMPLETION

Let us begin by looking back at Day 13 of our study where Moses and the Israelites were getting ready to leave Egypt. God instructed them to take a lamb without defect for each family, slaughter it, and place the blood on the "lintel and door posts." As you will recall the Israelites were attempting to exit Egypt, and Pharaoh, in spite of the nine plagues sent by God, would not release them. This was the 10th and final plague. God was going to strike every one of the first-born children in the land of Egypt. The only way that God's angel would know to "Passover" the Israelites house was by the blood of the lamb that covered the doorposts.

God said *"This will be a memorial day for you; you will celebrate it as a festival to God down through the generations, a fixed festival celebration to be observed always "*(Exodus 12:14). God went on to tell Moses: *"... when your children say to you, "Why are we doing this?' tell them: It's the Passover-sacrifice to God Who passed over the homes of* the *Israelites in Egypt when He hit Egypt with death but rescued us"* (Exodus 12:24-27). The significance of this event was that the very night that the Romans seized Jesus, our Perfect Lamb, in the garden is the beginning of the Passover Feast. Remember on day 37 we talked about Jesus eating the Passover meal with His disciples.

After His teaching and prayer in the garden, the Roman soldiers joined by the Jewish police took Jesus to the house of the Chief Priests. The next morning they took Jesus to a place where the religious leaders and high priests were gathered and brought Him before the High Council. From the High Council they took Jesus to Pilate. Read and highlight Luke 23:4 and record what Pilate told the crowd including the high priests in your Journal.

Pilate found nothing wrong with Him and told the crowd that since Jesus was a Galilean He was under Herod's jurisdiction. Therefore, they took Him to Herod. Read and highlight Luke 23:8-12 and record what took place there in your Journal.

Herod sent Jesus back to Pilate without a judgment because Jesus would say nothing. Turn to Matthew 27:15-26. Matthew's account does not talk about Herod, but it includes a couple of points of interest. First, you see Pilate's wife appealing to him in verse 19. Record what she says in your Journal.

Meanwhile the High Priests and religious leaders were convincing the crowd to pardon Barabbas instead of Jesus so they could have Him crucified. The next point of interest is when Pilate asks the crowd what they would want him to do to Jesus and they yell, *"Nail him to a cross!"* When Pilate asks them for what crime, the angry crowd yells louder *"Nail him to a cross!"* *"When*

Pilate saw that he was getting nowhere and that a riot was imminent, he took a basin of _____ and _____ his hands in full sight of the crowd, saying, "I'm washing my hands of _____ for this Man's death. From now on, it's in your _____. You're the _____ and _____." The crowd answered, "We'll take _____, we and our _____ after _____."

Those are strong words. Many of the Jewish people were convinced that Jesus' claims to be God were unfounded and because of that, they seethed with anger. They felt disconnected from God, but they knew what blasphemy was and they were not going to allow this man to say such things without appropriate action. They would settle for nothing less than crucifying Him. That is just what happened.

They made Him carry His cross on His beaten back to the final destination, Golgotha or "Skull Hill." They nailed Him to the cross after a lengthy beating. They stayed and watched Him until He took His last breath. Read and highlight Matthew 27:41-44. These men were ruthless. They did not believe that He was the Messiah. They stayed and taunted Jesus until He died.

Matthew records three significant events that took place upon Jesus' last breath. You can find them in Matthew 27:51-53: First, The Temple curtain ripped from top to bottom. The curtain separated the Holy Place from the Holy of Holies. (Look briefly at Hebrews 9:1-10.) It was a very thick piece of fabric that tore from top to bottom indicating that only God could have torn it. Perhaps the purpose of the tear was to demonstrate that the High Priests were no longer the only ones who had access to

God. Because of the sacrificial death and shed blood from the Unblemished Lamb, our Lord and Savior Jesus Christ, everyone now had access to God.

Second, an earthquake split rocks. Christ's death was an earthshaking event felt by all of creation. The final event that took place included tombs opening up and *"many bodies of Believers asleep in their graves were raised."* We do not know who they were or if anyone saw them.

I love what Matthew records in 27:54 After all of these things happened: *"The captain of the guard and those with him, when they saw the earthquake and everything else that was happening, were scared to death. They said,* '_____ _____ _____ _____ _____ _____ _____!"*

This is a monumental event in our Christian walk. The death of our Savior, as explained by the prophet Isaiah in his 53rd chapter, is an amazing event in the completion of God's perfect plan of redemption for believers.

We will explore the true completion of God's plan tomorrow. Please end today by telling our Lord how grateful you are for the pain He suffered to make us new.

MEMORIZATION

If you have come to the point that you can recite the Books of the Bible without making a mistake and without looking at your cards, then you have achieved your goal. However, just for fun, try it again, and this time, look at your watch or clock and time yourself. How much time did it take to get them all correct? Can you improve your time? Remember, this one is just for fun!

PRAYER OF AGREEMENT

Lord, my reader and I we stand expectantly today in a prayer of agreement for the souls of our loved ones (both family and friends). Thank You Holy Spirit for softening the hearts of our loved ones, and drawing them to You. Thank You in advance for saving them, in Jesus' mighty name, Amen.

Day 39

OPENING PRAYER

*L*ord, *I am eager to learn the things that You want to teach me today. Please open my heart and my mind as I prepare for Your lessons, and strengthen my ability to apply them in my life. In the name of Jesus I pray, Amen.*

LESSON: RESURRECTION

Let us take a little time to learn about the New Covenant before we move on to Jesus' Resurrection. Turn with me first to Jeremiah 31:31-32. Write word for word the second sentence in this passage in your Journal.

The Old Covenant that God had made with the Israelites required obedience to the law. Because the wages of sin is death, the Old Covenant required that people perform rituals and sacrifices in order to please God and remain in His grace. Read and highlight Hebrews 9:11-15. Record what the last sentence in this passage says in your Journal.

Jesus came and made this New Covenant "so we can live all out for God." He came to fulfill the law by obeying it perfectly. The righteousness that Jesus talked about was far different from what the Pharisees and teachers of the law knew. They were seeking external righteousness alone, but Jesus came so that we would have internal righteousness based on faith in God's Word. Look again at Jeremiah 31:33-34 and Hebrews 10:11-18.

The Old Covenant was written in stone. The New Covenant is written on our hearts.

Jesus was the ultimate sacrifice. Read and highlight Hebrews 10:19-25. The second sentence says *"Jesus has _____ the way by the _____ of his _____, acting as our priest before_____."* We are now given salvation as a free gift, not as a reward for our behavior. All we have to do is invite Jesus to live in our hearts and be our Savior. Once we are saved we share the permanent inheritance of God through Christ's redeeming blood.

Let us move on to Jesus' resurrection. One day my son David was deep in thought and suddenly he asked "Mom, what do you think the most important part of Jesus was… you know… was it His birth or His death or something else?" I thought about it for a moment and I said "probably His birth."

He said "not me, it was definitely His resurrection that I love the most, because it *completed* everything."

I stood in amazement at this nine-year-old boy who spoke with such wisdom. It was indeed an important event because it *completed* the work He was here to do.

Turn to the final chapter in the Book of Matthew. Jesus was placed in a tomb with a large stone rolled in front of the entrance. Mary Magdalene and Mary were present at the tomb when the ground shook and an angel came to them and told them that Jesus was raised *"just as he said."* The angel of God showed them the empty tomb and told them to go and tell the disciples (Matthew 28:7) *"He is risen from the dead. He is going on ahead of you to Galilee. You will see him there."* As they ran to tell the disciples, they met Jesus Who said *"Good Morning!"* What do the women do in verses 8-10?

Oh how the Lord loves it when we fall on our knees and worship him! Jesus told the women to tell His "brothers", also known as the disciples, to go to Galilee and wait for Him. Meanwhile, the religious leaders hear of Jesus' resurrection from the soldiers who were so scared they could not move. They decided to bribe the soldiers with a "large sum of money." They told the soldiers to tell people "His disciples came in the night and stole the body while we were sleeping." They assured the soldiers that they would not get in trouble for sleeping on the job. The Bible says, *"this story is still alive and active today."*

After Jesus' resurrection, He appeared to more than 500 people. It was exactly 40 days from His resurrection to His ascension. During this 40 days Jesus continued to teach. The last official commissioning Jesus gave the disciples is "The Great Commission." Turn to Matthew 28:18-20. Write word for word what Jesus told the disciples to do realizing that this commission is for us as well in your Journal.

I find comfort in the final words Jesus spoke.

He promised He would be with us every day until the very end. Stop and embrace the beauty of those words. I have such peace when I think that our Lord and Savior, Who came that we may have life everlasting, will be with us forever and ever. Write a prayer thanking Him for that promise and ask Him to give you strength to carry out The Great Commission.

MEMORIZATION

Without looking at your cards, can you tell me which Book of the Bible comes after Ruth? Now which one comes after Proverbs? Which one comes after Exodus? Which one comes before Galatians? Quiz yourself; you might be surprised how easily the answers come to you now.

PRAYER OF AGREEMENT

Lord, as we near the completion of our study together, we ask Your Holy Spirit to constantly and always abide with us and guide us in all Truth. May we always hear and discern Your voice, never stray from You, and always know the joy of being one with You and Your Spirit, day by day and hour by hour, in Jesus' name, Amen.

Day 40

OPENING PRAYER

*L*ord, as I complete this study today, I set myself to seek You, and I stand expectantly in faith that I will find You each and every day. As I continue throughout this day and my life to pursue You in prayer and in Your Word, I thank You that my walk with You is continuously being strengthened, and that my relationship to You is deepening each and every day for the rest of my life. In the name of Jesus I pray, Amen.

LESSON: ASCENSION OF CHRIST AND THE HOLY SPIRIT

We learn in Luke 24:50-51 that just before Jesus ascended into Heaven from Bethany, a village on the Mount of Olives, He raised his hands and blessed the disciples. Can you picture that amazing event?

Luke 24:52 says, *"they returned to Jerusalem bursting with joy."* It makes me "burst with joy" just to think about being blessed by Jesus in person. I would also be paralyzed and overcome with emotions. I would not want the moment to end. I would probably stay there staring into the sky recounting the events in my mind a thousand times. Luke tells us in Acts 1:9-11 that the disciples were doing exactly that. In fact, it took two angels to come along and snap them out of it!

The disciples and a number of Jesus' followers were in the upper room in Jerusalem on the day of Pentecost, which was the 50th day after the First Fruits Feast. Acts 2:1-4 tells us that the disciples were *"all together in one place"* when a *"strong wind, gale force"* came and like a *"wildfire, the Holy Spirit spread through their ranks and they started speaking in a number of different languages as the Spirit prompted them."*

Wind is the sign of God and fire is the symbol of His divine presence. God came into the room and His divine presence came upon every believer.

This event marked the beginning of the Church.

Peter was the first to speak about the events that took place. Acts 2:37 says that those who listened to Peter and the other apostles said, *"Brothers! Brothers! So now what do we do?"* Record Peter's response in your Journal:

The instructions are clear. This is what we are to do. The promises and instructions apply equally today, and to you and me. Let us end this study and our time together by reading, highlighting and meditating on Acts 3:12-26.

Do you see how we have come full circle from the first covenant? The time has come to do what Peter says in Acts 3:19-20: *"Now it's time to change your ways! Turn to face God so He can wipe away your sins, pour out showers of blessings to refresh you, and send you the Messiah He prepared for you, namely Jesus."*

It is time we live for Jesus so we can pass down a legacy of amazing faith.

Jesus is going to return one day. What a glorious day that will be. Until then, we have the opportunity to be the hands and feet of Christ by sharing the good news with others and helping them go deeper still.

End today, the final day of this study, proclaiming your intentions to ensure that God's Word will be practiced and taught in your home and in your life. Declare as Joshua did in Joshua 24:15: *"As for me and my family, we 'll worship God."*

MEMORIZATION

You made it to the end and I would like to congratulate you on a job well done. You might wish to keep your cards with you and review them from time to time, but you will also find as you study your Bible more and more that the names of the Books and the order they are in is etched into your mind and you will never forget them.

PRAYER OF AGREEMENT

Father, thank You for my reader who has now completed this study. Richly bless and prosper us as we continue to seek to know You in a deeper way for the rest of our lives. In the name of Jesus we pray, Amen.

Conclusion

I am so happy that you were dedicated enough to complete this Bible Study and I hope you gained a lot of valuable Bible knowledge along the way. If you did all of your memorizations, then you should have learned all of the Books of the Bible and you should be able to find any chapter when you need to read a certain scripture or verse. My heartfelt desire is that this book allowed you to learn things about the Bible that you did not know. I pray that this Bible Study creates a hunger in you to learn more about the Bible and about Jesus.

Do not stop just because you have come to the end of this Bible Study. Keep your spiritual guard up by staying in the Word. Put on your armor daily! Read your Bible daily. Read more Bible Studies. Join a group at your church and tithe regularly. Have a family Bible study.

I would also like to encourage you to share with others what you have learned through this study. Be an example to them. Share this book with them or give them a copy as an act of kindness. Never forget our Great Commission of sharing the Good News with others!

Author's Page

I am honored that you chose to read *Take me Deeper Still* and I hope that it has brought you closer to God. I wrote this book to bring myself closer to Him and to help me truly understand the Bible. My hope is that it has done the same for you. If you are interested in learning more about me and my life's mission, log on to Daphnez.com, visit my website at http://www.daphnez.com/or contact me by email at daphne@daphnez.com.

Blessings and love to you.

CPSIA information can be obtained
at www.ICGtesting.com
Printed in the USA
LVOW13s1046190417
531382LV00016B/357/P